ESCAPE FROM
NICOTINE
COUNTRY

ESCAPE FROM NICOTINE COUNTRY

HOW TO STOP SMOKING PAINLESSLY

JAMES CHRISTOPHER

Prometheus Books
59 John Glenn Drive
Amherst, New York 14228-2197

Published 1999 by Prometheus Books

Inquiries should be addressed to
Prometheus Books, 59 John Glenn Drive, Amherst, New York 14228–2197.
VOICE: 716–691–0133, ext. 207.
FAX: 716–564–2711.
WWW.PROMETHEUSBOOKS.COM

03 02 01 00 99   5 4 3 2 1

Library of Congress Cataloging-in-Publication Data

Christopher, James, 1942–
    Escape from nicotine country : how to stop smoking painlessly / James Christopher.
        p.   cm.
    Includes bibliographical references and index.
    ISBN 1–57392–751–1 (paper : alk. paper)
    1. Smoking cessation programs. 2. Cigarette habit—Treatment. I. Title.
HV5740.C48   1999
613.85—dc21   99–41267
                                                                         CIP

Printed in the United States of America on acid-free paper

Acknowledgments

Ranjit Sandhu is not only my exceptionally capable editor, he is also a caring friend who has long been supportive of my work in the recovery field. Ranjit heartily encouraged my premise that a recovery book could be fun, not dreary, and for that I am most grateful. Larry Beck, longtime friend and colleague, believed in my concept of a "smoker friendly" approach, contributing his formidable skills as a photographer to this project. Tom Genoni, a highly skilled graphic artist, provided cover art. I would also like to thank Martin Nicolaus and Jenifer Swan for their wonderful efforts in research for this project. Thanks again to one and all; your collective talents are what made this book possible.

Contents

THIS BOOK IS "SMOKER-FRIENDLY"!

Introduction

D ear Smoker,

Forty-six million adults in the U.S. currently smoke cigarettes and the trend among smokers is to *try to quit*; 25 percent of U.S. adults currently smoke, compared to 42.4 percent of the U.S. adult population who smoked in 1965.

Surveys indicate that *most* smokers (70 percent) *want* to stop smoking, although of the 34 percent who attempt to quit each year, only 2.5 percent are successful.

The scientific literature clearly establishes nicotine as a powerful drug of addiction, with neurobiological effects similar to those of most addictive drugs, and nicotine replacement therapy—as smoking-cessation treatment—necessitates a weaning-off process from the nicotine-replacement treatment *after* one stops smoking.

Surveys show that the majority of smokers lack the interest, need, and resources to seek formal cessation treatment, thus *Escape from Nicotine Country* provides a simple, supportive, economical "how to" self-empowerment approach to quit comfortably without tedious "programs" and expensive treatments.

I've striven to make this book as "smoker-friendly" as possible; by that I mean straightforward and immediately useful without a lot of superfluous crap. The prospect of stopping smoking is scary as hell. I know—I've been there. Nicotine addiction is ultimately painful, therefore this book offers a gradual smoking-cessation approach to stop the addiction painlessly, without weight gain.

This work is purposely structured to get to the point quickly, because human life is at stake here and there's no time to waste. Chapters 1 through 6 are designed to give you all the preparatory information you need in order to comfortably carry out Plan A, B, or C, as presented in chapter 7.

After achieving your first nicotine-free day—and your first ninety days of a nicotine-free life (chapter 8)—the Logbook continues day-by-day through your first year of freedom from nicotine (chapter 9). Chapter 10 offers tobacco-free musings, and some stuff for the future.

References/Resources

In the back of this book you will find listings of the scientific sources upon which I based these strategies. And you will also find a wealth of supportive resources and referrals for building a new smoke-free life.

One Smoker's Story:
An Overview

Tobacco is a dirty weed: I like it.
It satisfies no normal need: I like it.
It makes you thin, it makes you lean,
It takes the hair right off your bean;
It's the worst darn stuff I've ever seen:
    I like it.
      —Graham Hemminger (1896–1949), *Tobacco*

This sentiment, to my mind, brilliantly sums up addiction at its core: "Who cares about the consequences? I want my drug!"

There are various ways to address addiction; I discovered one by accident over twenty-one years ago and haven't wanted an alcoholic beverage since. I later applied this powerful method to my smoking addiction of over thirty years and haven't wanted a cigarette since.

11

I arrested my debilitating addiction to booze at a time (April 24, 1978) when smoking was still "fashionable." I continued to smoke until November 26, 1993. As I smoked in sobriety, along with lots of company in the earlier years, I was, as I had been in the case with my previously active alcoholism, unaware in any real way of my *addiction* to cigarettes or of its negative consequences. I knew how to "do sobriety," but hadn't yet made "the connection" concerning my nicotine addiction.

Making the connection—replacing the "cycle of addiction" with a new "cycle of sobriety"—was what I'd termed "the Sobriety Priority" back in 1988, when my first book about recovery from alcoholism was published. I had founded a new self-help support group movement earlier in 1986, after articles I'd written addressing the need for alternatives in the recovery world had received international attention and positive response. SOS, or Save Our Selves, self-empowerment groups sprang up nationwide and ultimately worldwide. Thousands of addicts have utilized the powerful yet simple SOS method for achieving and maintaining freedom from alcohol and other drugs.

As the years advanced, I didn't, as far as stopping smoking was concerned. My denial mechanism manifested itself in this way: "I smoke only one-half to one pack per day. I see no negative consequences as a result of my smoking. I eat healthful foods and exercise a bit. I have loads of fulfillment—some downs, but who doesn't? I'm a courteous smoker. I have no history of cancer (although ample history of heart trouble, but only on one side of my family). My real addiction is to alcohol and isn't it great to be living sober, etc?"

"I only smoke socially," I quipped to the relatively few folks who approached me concerning my addiction to nicotine. The *real* reason I smoked was that I was hooked and afraid to experience life without my cigarettes. I had a real gut-level (primal) dependency on cigarettes. I needed the feeling I got from smoking for my quality of life—strike that—for *my life*. Yes, I needed this, I felt in my deepest core, below my conscious level of recognition, *in order to survive!*

A controversial addiction-treatment professional had said to me long ago—knowing of my work in the field of alcoholism, and how apparently effective the Sobriety Priority approach had been both in my life and in the lives of thousands of addicted individuals—that addiction is an affliction "of the survival system of the individual." This profound truth—which I had ultimately discovered by accident almost twenty years earlier, had, through trial and error, set me free from active alcoholism.

And, as I developed my "sobriety priority" approach early in my recovery, I felt comfortable and secure in my sobriety *as a separate issue from all else*. It didn't matter what happened in my life or what other people said or did to shake or challenge my personal heartfelt truth. I *knew* passionately both in my gut and *simultaneously* in my mind that I could not ingest alcohol with impunity: I could not drink alcohol or use other mind-altering drugs and *get away with it*. So as others struggled with sobriety, I did not. I had been freed from a knee-jerk reaction to drink.

Smoking? That's something else again, I told myself; after all, it's not really a mind-altering drug. Sure, people probably shouldn't smoke, I suppose, but I'm a light smoker. I suffer no consequences as a result of my smoking, so leave me alone; I don't want to think about that right now. And so it went for years.

Tragically, when it comes to the ingestion of harmful addictive drugs, the primal survival system that should reject that which is harmful and accept that which is not, innocently accepts any ingested drug that offers an immediate euphoric rush. Our bodies want more, becoming ultimately off-balance and chemically dependent.

Eventually all else takes a backseat to the survival system's primitive perception. The interpretation conveyed and accepted *without ques-*

tion in chemical language—the language of "feel good" or "feel bad," survive/thrive or cease to exist—by the primal core of the individual human organism is, in the case of harmful drugs, unfortunately a lie. There is typically no negative chemical message immediately following the feel-good chemical "OK." There is only an immediate positive feeling of pleasure.

Typically there is a gap, a space or span of time, no connection—no chemical "aha!" process. There is no chemical mechanism that informs one's primitive survival system of the inherent danger of ingesting addictive substances that feel good immediately upon ingestion.

Survival systems don't compute; they don't deal with concepts or consequences. Unless the experience renders an *immediate* rather than a *delayed* hurtful response (like touching a hot stove, for instance) it is accepted, chemically speaking, as positive and life-affirming; therein lies the reason for the addict's obvious self-destructive, irrational, addictive behavior.

Since there is no rationality available in the primitive part of the psyche, the connection that drug = hurt from later consequences is not made. Hangovers for alcohol abusers? No connection. Coughing up blood for nicotine addicts? No connection.

On rare occasions, the individual human organism can experience a head/gut "fusion" of chemical "language" or an awareness that simultaneously floods the brain. This powerful occurrence typically happens accidentally, if at all (as it had in my own alcoholism).

Fortuitously in a flash moment, in a flashing glimpse of my own mortality—I experienced alcohol = *immediate pain* in immediate chemical language: "Alcohol hurts immediately"; the deeper survival-of-the-organism core message being: "Alcohol kills!" Chemical conclusion and rational conscious conclusion: alcohol (for me) = death; sobriety (for me) = life.

Although my powerful "sobriety priority" experience came about accidentally, the good news, I discovered, is that this *can* be a *deliberately induced process!* Although this book is not about alcoholism, I've briefly related my own alcoholism addiction-arrest experience for clarity. I also think it is noteworthy to state that alcohol is considered by most researchers in the field of addiction to be a *selectively* addictive drug; that is, approximately 10 percent of those who ingest alcohol become addicted. Nicotine, however, has been found to hook virtually all those who use it, if they repeat the initial behavior.

"More addictive than heroin," concludes the scientific literature concerning nicotine. I became aware of the facts about nicotine addiction and the consequences related to its habitual use over time, but I didn't really apply the horrors of nicotine addiction to myself until *after* I made a decision to attempt to "get real" about my cigarette smoking. Not being fond of pain and having experienced a comfortable sobriety for a good number of years, I set out to create an approach to stop smoking that wouldn't be painful.

Fantasies of Hollywood's double-cigaretted Paul Henreid and Bette Davis from the film *Now Voyager* (1942), in which Henreid lights two cigarettes simultaneously, then hands one to Davis as their eyes transfix, fed the flames of my long-skewed perspective on smoking.

Developing an Escape Plan

When I decided to attempt to quite smoking, I really didn't known if my efforts would succeed. I was hopeful as I informally planned to give it a try. I told no one.

I decided that my typical smoking day for a twenty-four-hour period consisted of about twenty cigarettes. (I had smoked more in earlier years due to the "synergistic" combination of alcohol and cigarettes.) I simply made a note of this in my date book as I planned for "day one" to begin the following morning. I allowed myself a standard pack of filtered king-size cigarettes as my allotment for "day one" (although I have smoked many different brands over the years, both filtered and unfiltered—as with booze earlier in my life, I had consumed countless brands of beer, wine, bourbon, scotch, vodka, etc.).

My plan was to *gradually* cease, to make it easy on myself. I'd heard too many stories of smokers struggling to quit, suffering withdrawal symptoms, stuffing their faces with food as an oral substitute only to return to smoking, sporting additional pounds, demoralized.

I didn't want to suffer needless agony, nor did I want to embrace my refrigerator in order to compensate for my loss. I'd always had hearty appetites: booze (in the past), cigarettes, good food, stimulating relationships and activities. I knew that typically the average person who stops smoking tends to gain approximately five pounds, but this weight gain generally levels off in a short time. A main reason for weight gain is nicotine's role in suppressing hunger and eating. Smokers tend to weigh less than nonsmokers, that is, the weight of smokers is *artificially controlled via nicotine addiction.*

I didn't want to feel deprived.

I didn't want to hurt or get fat.

This was my challenge.

As stated earlier, I smoked my last cigarette on November 26, 1993. It was a Friday and one cigarette was all that I could comfortably tolerate. Saturday the 27th, in the midst of hectic work-related travel, while staying at the home of a married couple (one of whom consistently smoked cigars), I calmly walked downstairs to join them and a group of outdoors smokers in the couple's backyard, *with no nicotine cravings whatsoever* on my first cigaretteless day.

At that moment I felt liberated. I had arrested a nicotine addiction of over thirty years, painlessly. I experienced no feeling of loss; I felt instead that I'd escaped from a kind of slavery. And I wanted this feeling of freedom to last a lifetime.

"My name is Jim. I'm a sober alcoholic. I keep my nicotine addiction arrested also. I don't drink alcohol or smoke cigarettes, no matter what."

No, this is not a "twelve-step" statement; nor is it a statement regarding my willpower or character. *As a separate issue from all else*, it is a factual life-and-death statement about maintaining the survival of an organism, namely me. It is not only conceptualized in my head as I say it; it is *simultaneously* felt in my gut.

The fortuitous accident that happened to me over twenty-one years ago regarding my addiction to booze, that is, my aforementioned "mortality moment" in which, apparently, I experienced what I now call "cognitive/visceral synchronization," was a kind of fusion, if you will, a simultaneous head-and-gut realization; an "organic," "holistic" jolt. This had been a profound, seemingly beyond words, "aha!" experience, in which one sees (meaning conceptualizes and feels at the same time), something along these lines: "This is real! This shit is killing me! I've got to stop this now, *no matter what!*"

This moment of brain/gut clarity was, of course, only my beginning. But it was a hell of a jump-start upon which I built, *through deliberately induced procedures*, a remarkably comfortable booze-free existence where, previously, I had deteriorated to the point of existing only to drink. I had also previously attempted an almost-successful suicide and had, through alcoholism, almost given up on my life.

Later, after years of "separate-issue sobriety," I discovered that the procedures I'd developed earlier, originating from my "aha!" experience regarding my alcoholism, worked beautifully when *deliberately* applied to my nicotine addiction, with some modifications.

Modifications, options, tools, stuff that you can pick and choose and utilize, as derived from the suggestions in this book, will provide you with a way out of your nicotine addiction. You can apply the simple, straightforward procedures put forth in this book to create your very own personal approach, constructed by you and for you, specifically to empower you to arrest your nicotine addiction comfortably and not gain weight in the process.

So what happened in the twenty days prior to my first cigaretteless day in beautiful Sylmar, California? I've located the notes in my old date book. My personal smoking-cessation plan was deliberately designed not to be oppressive. What do I mean by that? Simply this: I wanted to continue doing whatever I was doing at that particular time in my life without additional burdens, stress, or tedious "programs" to follow.

My plan, as it pertained to smoking cigarettes, was to begin on "Day One" with an allotment of twenty cigarettes—spaced throughout the day—morning, afternoon, and evening—as I chose. On "Day Two" I would reduce my allotment of cigarettes to nineteen. "Day Three" to eighteen, and so on until "DAY TWENTY," when I was to smoke my final cigarette.

Knowing that sometimes people eat when they're simply thirsty, possibly dehydrated, rather than genuinely hungry, I planned to drink two liters of liquid a day, generally recommended as a healthful practice. A variety of delicious sugar-free, fat-free beverages including fresh water were, and are, readily available.

I was already adept at "making calories count," that is, I enjoyed eating heartily without weight gain. I had accomplished this for some years by recreating all the delicious foods that I loved in reduced-fat versions of their original recipes. For instance, it was easy to quickly prepare virtually fat-free versions of cheeseburgers and fries, topped off with pie and ice cream. I kept sugar-free chewing gum (some smoking-cessation professionals specifically recommend spicy cinnamon-flavored sugarless gum) and sugar-free lollipops along with other sugar-free, fat-free hard candies readily available. I had cinnamon sticks, toothpicks, carrot sticks, and celery stalks around too. I bought a couple of inexpensive smooth stones from a lapidary shop so that I'd have something to do with my potentially restless heretofore cigarette-clutching hands. I took leisurely walks daily. I began to add little extras, like climbing the stairs rather than taking escalators in shopping malls. Again, none of these procedures was oppressive, obsessive, or tedious. My stamina began to improve, my energy level increased.

After completing twenty days of gradual smoking cessation, I comfortably began DAY ONE of my new smoke-free life. I continued these simple strategies and gradually felt a lessened interest in chewing gum, toothpicks, etc., and an increased interest in fitness activities as my lungs cleared and I began to feel more fit.

Earlier I mentioned the application of *deliberately induced* "cognitive/visceral synchronization" procedures. These were simple "get real/stay real" slogans, distilled from negative personal experience concerning nicotine addiction.

In my case, I'd never had heavy-duty negatives caused directly by my smoking. I'd not coughed up blood, or suffered from "smoker's cough" for that matter. But upon reflection, I easily found some "get real" material to use: Sometimes, after smoking a cigarette, I'd feel fatigued and standing up would make me dizzy. I also recalled some pretty "gawd-awful" tastes in my mouth due to smoking.

One day, after some time in my new cigarette-free life, I had quite a powerful and moving experience related to my freedom from addiction to cigarettes. I was standing in line at a supermarket, something I'd done countless times before, but this time the huge display rack of numerous brands of cigarettes caught my attention. I said to myself, silently, with tears of confrontation welling up in my eyes as I directly addressed that cigarette display rack, "You addicted me for thirty years! Damn you!"

This may seem a bit dramatic, and clearly it isn't everyone's cup of tea. I suppose that's the point. These are very personal issues. Material impacts each of us with varying levels of intensity. In choosing "get real" material, each individual's experiences and sense memories will be unique. Moreover, some deliberately induced "aha!" experiences may develop a depth of meaning gradually, rather than suddenly. Sense memories can be powerful tools for recovery from addiction.

Made famous by Constantin Stanislavski's "method" acting techniques taught over sixty years ago in the Moscow Art Company, sense-memory techniques are utilized by our most esteemed actors today. When we experience a moment in a film or on the stage that "feels real," it, in effect, *is* real. That's because the actor we are watching has super-imposed his or her own personal sense memory (that is, the *emotional* memory of an event from the actor's own life) onto the "feelings" of the character being portrayed in the film or play; thus, when the actor cries or expresses other emotions, it seems real because it, indeed, *is* real.

There are many ways to call up real, emotion-laden negative memories concerning one's smoking addiction. A few moments of reflection in your early days of recovery (there's no need to obsess on this procedure) will call up things that you don't like about your smoking. You might feel generally sad about the impact of cigarettes on your life. There's material there. And, in getting real, you need not exaggerate or embellish. Why? Because in our heart of hearts we each know what is true for us individually, and in applying these procedures, you will ultimately only be able to *accept* what is true in regard to arresting your addiction.

Let me be clear: This is *not* a self-deprecating process. No human being ever intended to get chemically hooked. Addiction damages our *precious* human survival systems. Someone who has had an addiction experience is different, altered from those who have not. The addict's natural survival system has sustained damage. We cannot cure our addictions. But we *can* arrest an addiction, and keep it arrested, by comfortably reclaiming our very own survival systems.

A Special Note . . .

A few years ago, while doing research for this project, I purchased a book from the American Council on Science and Health. Later, unbeknownst to me, my publisher, Prometheus Books, acquired the aforementioned work and published it under the title, *Cigarettes: What the Warning Label Doesn't Tell You.* This astonishing book contains twenty eye-opening chapters—all carefully reviewed by independent health experts—explaining clearly and honestly how cigarette smoking can affect the body from head to toe, far beyond the obvious risks of heart disease, lung cancer and emphysema, stroke, and concerns over second-hand smoke. Probed in depth are conditions few would even associate with smoking—risks to which moderate to light smokers are susceptible: blood vessel disease, skin disease and wrinkles, risks during surgery, joint and bone problems, pediatric illness, male infertility and impotence, nerve disorders, numerous types of cancer, depression, hearing loss, eye disorders, Crohn's disease, and more. I urge you to contact Prometheus Books directly by phone or mail (Prometheus Books, 59 John Glenn Drive, Amherst, New York 14228–2197; tel. 716–691–0133; fax. 716–691–0137) and to purchase this book a.s.a.p. so that you can utilize it as a valuable "get real/stay real" tool during your personal recovery process from nicotine addiction. I receive absolutely no remuneration of any kind for this, nor is this my publisher's idea; it is entirely my idea. I placed this recommendation here, at the end of chapter 1, because some people never read introductions to books, and I feel strongly about the educational value of this informative work.

WHAT'S <u>YOUR</u> STORY?

Square One:
Sharing Your
Personal Smoking Story

I'll go first. When I was about nineteen years old, and a theatre arts student at the University of Texas in Austin, I reveled in the knowledge that those jerks majoring in our perceived rival department, namely radio and television broadcasting, thought us weird. I started dressing "theatrically," wearing a beret and toying with an overpriced brand of cigarettes called Vogue. As I recall, these filtered smokes came in a choice of multicolors or black with gold tips. I was enormously cool and the fancy cigarettes played a significant role in my coolness. Soon enough I was smoking for real and didn't look back. I eventually dumped the overpriced smokes and switched to more conventional brands.

So how and when and where did you start smoking? What were

the circumstances, as best you can recall, and how did you feel at the time? Pick up your pen and start writing. Use additional sheets of paper, if necessary.

_____

_____

_____

_____

_____

_____

_____

_____

_____

_____

_____

_____

_____

_____

_____

_____

_____

As they say in support groups: "Thank you for sharing." But you're not done yet. In the privacy of your own place, situate yourself in front of a mirror and read your personal story aloud to yourself while glancing into the mirror as often as possible. This helps make your smoking story more impactful to you, thus launching your awareness in the "get real about smoking" process. After completing this procedure, go on to chapter 3.

THIS S--T
IS KILLING ME!

Let's Get Real:
Recalling, Acknowledging, and Accepting Your Very Own "Cigarette Burns"

As I said earlier, cognitive/visceral synchronization is a name I dreamed up to describe an impactful realization that I personally experienced over twenty-one years ago, which freed me at last from active alcohol addiction. It simply denotes a cognitive "aha!" experience, a lightbulb-over-the-head circumstance, coupled with a *simultaneous* gut feeling; thus a "full body understanding," if you will. Thinking *and* feeling in the same awareness moment: "This is real! This shit is killing me! I've got to stop this now, *no matter what!*" may *not* occur as readily to a smoker as to one addicted to alcohol or any of the other severely mind-bending drugs. Why? Because until relatively recently cigarette smoking was considered "the norm," an "OK," "cool" thing to do. Glamorized. Sanitized. Part of the landscape. At worst, an annoying habit. Tobacco corporation CEOs stood before members of the U.S. Congress during the 1990s and stated, man for man, with straight faces, that nicotine wasn't an addictive substance.

After all, some of our greatest achievers have been smokers. Smoking generally doesn't cause one to drive a car over an embankment or tear families apart. Dynamic dads and marvelous moms have smoked. Brilliant college students have enjoyed cigarette breaks, unimpaired, graduating with highest honors. Lovers tenderly stroke and smoke.

Although this stuff is true, we now know some new stuff and can take a more informed look:

- Many life-ending maladies have their roots in nicotine addiction.
- Countless little Debbies and little Billies have been impacted by and even died from secondhand smoke.
- Virtually all smokers would start sweating if someone suddenly took their stash away.

Sure, some smokers are courteous, careful, concerned. They only smoke outdoors, not in the home or family car or the workplace.

So what? Smokers are addicted to the drug they smoke and so . . .

As a fellow nicotine addict with an arrested addiction, I offer you tools and straightforwardly say to you: These tools will aid you in escaping from nicotine country and in reclaiming a smoke-free life painlessly, without unwanted weight gain.

Now, let's personally recall some real stuff that dreams aren't made of that directly comes from smoking cigarettes.

I'll go first. I never coughed up blood. I passed a doctor's lung test with "flying colors" toward the end of my smoking. I seemed to have stamina even though I smoked. My relationships with others, smokers and nonsmokers alike, seemed fine.

But . . . I began to gradually realize via societal attitudes growing harsher re: smoking, and via the advent of smoking-awareness campaigns, that my smoking was really an oppressive addiction. Eventually, I wanted to want to stop. Different stuff is impactful to different folks; for instance, I'd heard that you get your taste for food back and that your lungs clear up and so forth, but for me the really impactful stuff was my growing resentment at being dependent on a drug that brought me bad stuff along with my nicotine fix. I began to allow these items into my awareness: I looked at my dizziness; my fatigue, which I'd come to accept as a norm for over thirty smoke-filled years; my watery eyes and the toxic tastes in my mouth. I began to explore, rather than continue to deny, the reality of my addiction. Through my research, I learned:

- Nicotine is a stimulant, but the drug suppresses emotional awareness, resulting in depression and low self-esteem.
- The addicted brain experiences smoking as beneficial and the loss of cigarettes as a threat.

I also learned that health consequences of smoking include, but are not limited to, high blood pressure, heart disease, heart attack, diabetes, allergies, dental problems, asthma, emphysema, pregnancy problems, hoarseness, hyperglycemia, excess sweating, upset stomach, eye irritation, cough, ulcer, stroke, sinusitis, dizziness, heart palpitation, chest pains, nervousness, swelling of limbs, shortness of breath, low energy, poor circulation, sexual malfunctions, dulled sense of smell and taste, acid stomach and indigestion, sleeplessness.

I came to see that wrinkling skin, more frequent colds and flu, cigarette burns on clothing and furniture, the high cost of cigarettes, increased insurance rates, cigarette breath, stained teeth and fingers, growing social unacceptability, decreased stamina, dirty ashtrays, the stale smell of smoke on my clothing and in my home and car were never featured in pro-smoking ads that cost cigarette companies billions of dollars a year.

Pick up your pen and list your very own "cigarette burns," that is, your compelling reasons for quitting that you *feel* as you *think* about them:

MY PERSONAL SMOKING REALITY LIST

_____
_____
_____
_____
_____
_____
_____
_____
_____

Now that you've listed at least some of the reasons cigarette smoking makes you feel bad (you can add to the list whenever new stuff occurs to you), position yourself in front of your mirror and say something like this:

"My name is _____ and I acknowledge and accept that my addiction to cigarettes has resulted in _____." Insert selections from your personal smoking-reality list here while glancing in the mirror as often as possible.

Continue your "mirror work" by saying, "I feel _____." State what you feel now while looking directly at yourself in your mirror and, to add to your growing awareness of smoking consequences, read daily portions of the book I suggested at the end of chapter 1. Dr. C. Everett Koop, former U.S. Surgeon General, calls it "an authoritative—and chilling—account of what happens when you smoke."

Go on to chapter 4.

I'M PERFECTLY RATIONAL. GIVE ME A #@*¡%$ CIGARETTE!

When "I Want to Want to Stop Smoking" Becomes, Simply, "I Want to Stop Smoking"

I don't know about you, but I'm not fond of pain. Wouldn't it be great if things were reversed, concerning cigarette addiction; that is, what if smoking hurt instantly, like sticking your fingers into a blazing fire would hurt? Or, what if the inside of your mouth, nose, sinuses, throat, and lungs hurt instantly, as if they'd all been simultaneously seared by hot branding irons (perhaps imprinting "nicotine country" onto your gums, down your throat, and across your lungs)? That sort of instantaneous reaction, if it were possible, would make cigarette smoking less desirable, even though each "hit" or "drag" off a cigarette offers a nicotine "fix," reaching the brain in seven seconds, twice as fast as a syringe of heroin injected into the vein.

In a way, one's chemical addiction is like the proverbial bear-and-honey scenario: The bear doesn't understand that the numerous painful bee-sting attacks are a direct result of its recent theft of the honey and so it will continue to endure this pain, over and over, for life. But—and picture here a big bear *butt*—*Homo Sapiens* have not only (in common with our bear buddies as well as reptiles, amphibians, and fish) the ever-popular "limbic system": a ring of cerebral cortex, the oldest portion of the cortex, now thought to control various emotional and behavioral patterns . . . we human folk *also* have *highly developed* frontal-lobe potential (unlike our bear buddies' frontal-lobe potential) going for us as well. And, yet another *but*: our "lizard brains" or primitive limbic systems know nothing of "right" or "wrong" or "character" or "resolve"; our primitive survival mechanism of fight-or-flight, accept-or-reject, interprets nicotine (or heroin for that matter) as "good" in chemical/emotional language because it feels good immediately. Consequences be damned when addiction sets in.

Here's an interesting question: Would nicotine addicts steal car radios, lie, cheat, and the like, if smokes were illegal, underground?

Now that we're (almost) done with buts, let me state that we human guys and gals have the equipment to escape from nicotine country painlessly, unlike bears, who, lovable as they may be, when it comes to the perils of obtaining honey, just don't "get it" regarding their learned "cycle of need."

We humans, however, can "get it," albeit, we had better respect our very (underscore *very*) *powerful* primitive parts *as much as* we do our newer "reasoning equipment," i.e., our frontal lobes. If we humans could simply react "rationally" to addictive chemicals, specifically nicotine, one could—perhaps while on horseback, trotting through nicotine country—sensibly utter something like this: "Cigarette smoking is not in my best interest" and confidently ride into the sunset, nicotineless. But (again with the but) virtually all ye who puff the cigs for a while, *become hooked*. I did for a fair amount of time—30 years. Of course, there are exceptions. I knew a woman once who apparently wasn't hooked on cigarettes, smoking only occasionally, when she chose to do so. Naturally, classically, addicts will think (if you can call it thinking), "I could be one of those rare exceptions!"

BUT, with cigarettes, even occasional smoking has been found to be hazardous to your health! And if you are one of the so-called lucky ones who can "take it or leave it" you probably wouldn't be reading this book. Let's get on with it.

I have modified the following material from one of my previous alcohol-addiction recovery books, *Unhooked: Staying Sober and Drug-Free* (Prometheus Books, 1989), specifically to address nicotine drug addiction, rather than alcohol drug addiction:

The Cycle of Addiction

The simple procedures offered in this book for achieving and maintaining freedom from nicotine addiction are cognitive/visceral (or "head/ gut") synchronization strategies. They can be applied whenever you wish to prevent relapse.

This approach respects the power of "nature" (genetic inheritance, progressive addiction processes) and of "nurture" (learned habits, behaviors, and associations) by showing how to achieve the initial arrest of nicotine addiction and to keep your nicotine addiction arrested.

The "cycle of addiction" contains three debilitating elements: *chemical need* (at the physiological cellular level),

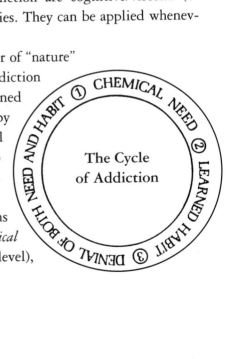

learned habit (chronic behaviors and associations), and *denial* of both need and habit.

The cycle of nicotine addiction becomes "second nature," automatically accepted as a way of life.

The Cycle of Recovery

The cycle of addiction can be successfully replaced by another cycle: *the cycle of recovery*. This cycle contains three essential elements: *acknowledgment* of your addiction to nicotine; *acceptance* of your addiction; and *prioritization* of recovery procedures to replace the addiction.

The daily cognitive/visceral application of your new recovery procedures arrests the cycle of addiction. It frees you to experience "everything else," by teaching you to associate "everything else" with recovery, not with addiction-driven behaviors. The cycle of recovery remains in place only so long as you choose to continue to acknowledge the existence of your arrested addiction. An addict's addiction is either active or arrested. This is your lifelong reality.

When you begin your personal smoking-cessation plan, you could say something like the following every day: "My name is _____. I acknowledge that cigarette smoking is an addiction. I accept that I cannot smoke cigarettes, no matter what I may think, experience, feel. My recovery is my first priority, and it is a separate issue from everything else in my life."

Another affirmation could go like this: "My name is _____. I am a nicotine addict. I cannot and do not smoke cigarettes or use any other tobacco products, no matter what. I can't smoke and get away with it. My recovery is my priority, and an issue separate from all else." Both versions express acknowledgment, acceptance, and prioritization.

These personal cognitive/visceral or "head/gut" affirmations have more impact when experienced as "mirror work." Even when a mirror is not available, you can repeat these "get real/stay real" statements of truth to yourself at any time, anywhere you wish, once you begin your smoking-cessation plan.

The recovery priority, applied daily, gradually weakens smoking associations, halting the cycle of addiction and allowing time for new associations to form as you experience your life free from cigarettes. As you continue to "make peace" with the facts regarding your arrested addiction—that is, as you continue to recognize smoking as a *non*option—you will come to *prefer* a cigarette-free lifestyle; you will long to preserve it, to respect your arrested addiction, to protect your new life.

Acknowledgment

Smoking stopped working for me. The price for my pleasure-center fix became too high. I glimpsed my mortality in a real blood-and-guts, finite way and my romanticized dream-views fell apart. It was then that I acknowledged I was hooked on cigarettes. I accepted that I could not stop smoking once I started. It occurred to me that if I stopped and "stayed stopped," no matter what came my way, it would probably be better than my then-current life situation. And it was.

Through this acknowledgment of my nicotine addiction, I began to desire to protect and maintain my new life. I wanted freedom from the bondage of my cycle of addiction.

I take responsibility for my own recovery. I respect my arrested addiction. As I continue to stay free from cigarettes, I think well of myself for my achievement. The very act of staying free from cigarettes gives me self-esteem. Every day I credit myself for my continuing recovery. You must acknowledge addiction to smoking as your here-and-now reality in order to begin your recovery.

Acceptance

Who among us really wants to accept that he or she has an addiction? Does an injured combat vet gleefully accept that he no longer has legs?

But acceptance is necessary to recovery. One has first to acknowledge, then accept, facts that can no longer be denied. Denial can go on for years, and many persons die while in the process.

When the combat vet awakens each morning, he experiences the fact that he no longer has legs. Not so with addicts. We must reacknowledge and reaccept our arrested addictions. We have no motorized wheelchair gleaming in a bedroom corner to remind us to acknowledge and accept. Our reminder must be a head/gut thing in order to keep our addiction arrested.

Some of us go through a brief period of mourning. We seem to have lost an old friend in quitting smoking. The phenomenon, as far as I am concerned, is similar to that of a hostage coming to identify with his terrorist captor. Called "the Stockholm Syndrome," it's normal for some—but of course it's completely irrational. Eventually, we come to prefer a life of freedom from cigarettes, and that joyous realization is a pleasure to contemplate.

Prioritization as a Separate Issue

Once you have acknowledged and accepted the reality of your addiction, once you have really stopped denying your addiction, doesn't prioritizing recovery make sense? Simply put, prioritizing your recovery means:

1. You choose to value that which affords you a life.
2. Your recovery is an *untouchable* separate issue. Smoking is not an option for you, because you are addicted to smoking, that is, you cannot smoke with impunity; you cannot smoke *and get away with it*.
3. As long as you continue to restate this commitment to yourself, acknowledging and accepting who you are, you're set free to experience everything else.

"Everything else" means that you can get angry, anxious, fearful, joyous, sad, thrilled, nervous, stressed, bored, jealous, intimate, and happy—experience the full gamut of your emotions—without fearing that you are in a "relapse mode." Connecting recovery to necessary emotional states is risky business. Connecting it to the realization that you simply can't smoke makes a lot more sense. This approach fits the evidence; it's a lot less confusing, and it *works*.

"Everything else" also means you can be a rascal, a pauper, a king, a democrat, a republican, a libertarian, a fascist, a socialist, or combinations of any of the above, and *still stay free from cigarettes*.

In recovery, as each new day passes, we brush our teeth, comb our hair, succeed, fail, laugh, cry, argue, learn, experience setbacks, feel pain, think dark thoughts, regret losses, pity ourselves, accept ourselves, dislike ourselves, and experience highs and lows. And in recovery, this all becomes new, as if done for the first time. Every day is a victory.

When we smoke, we tamper with our delicate neurological balance. Many times this alteration seems to be of minimal consequence; however, addiction to nicotine takes on a life of its own, and we literally become secondary, slaves, as the feeding of our "needy cells" becomes our number-one priority.

Scientists say that *Homo sapiens* is genetically programmed to be a creature of habit. When we learn things, we in a sense "own" them. Behavior is imprinted onto our brains, to be called up when related associations come along. For cigarette addicts, smoking tends to be associated with just about everything.

In my smoking days, for example, I associated smoking with butterfly wings, turkey legs, neon signs, world peace, good times, bad times, creativity, pathos, inhaling, exhaling, making dinner, making love—just about everything. My cigarette-to-mouth reflexes would operate "faster than my neurotransmitters could fire," as one friend said to me.

However, addiction can be arrested, and associations can be weakened.

When viewing smoking from the cellular-addictive standpoint, two points emerge:

1. Once the cells are freed from cigarettes, it becomes crucial to keep these cells away from cigarettes.
2. If smokers smoke again, the cells will be "waiting" for their chemical fix. The original addiction is once again fired up. Cellular need, primitive need, does not request compliance—it demands it.

If you now simply want to stop smoking, move on to chapter 5.

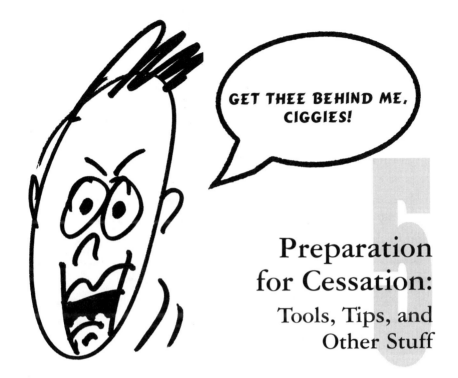

GET THEE BEHIND ME, CIGGIES!

Preparation for Cessation:
Tools, Tips, and Other Stuff

Some informal activity is in order as you gear up for your escape from nicotine country. You might begin by taking a ride to the local shopping mall, parking your car a bit farther from the entrance than you normally do and using the stairs, rather than the escalator. Stop by the candy store and stock up on fat-free/sugar-free treats of all stripes: hard candies, lollipops, jelly bellies, etc. Don't forget cinnamon sticks, slow-melting jawbreakers, and sugar-free gum. Walk on over to the supermarket for toothpicks, carrot sticks, celery stalks, and other crunchy fresh vegetables. Load up on bottled water and sugar-free soda pop. Visit the lapidary shop for a couple of smooth stones or go to the novelty store for marbles to tumble in your hands, or purchase a small flexi-plastic stress bag to squeeze.

Start getting used to utilizing these items; acquaint yourself with the feel of them.

Pop over to the bookstore and check out two sections: "Nutrition," for good cookbooks featuring reduced-fat and fat-free recipes for home preparation of your favorite foods, and "Fitness," for a moderate exercise-at-home book, preferably illustrated, with easy-to-execute movements. Pull out your pocket planner or mark your wall calendar with a "start date" to commence your smoking-cessation plan.

Now, put in a call to inform your family doctor about your decision to shortly begin a "taper" (gradual reduction) smoking-cessation plan, including your start date. Your doctor can be a valuable ally in your efforts.

Complete this chapter and chapter 6, then move on to chapter 7, choosing either plan A, B, or C, as it pertains to your personal smoking-addiction history, and begin.

The balance of this chapter will address questions you might have about all the stuff we've covered previously, as well as new supportive self-help/self-empowerment strategies that aren't too scary, so that you're not subjected to an unnecessarily "bumpy ride" on the road to recovery. If you wish, go ahead and peek at the smoking-cessation plans in chapter 7, then finish the material in this chapter.

Smart Eating That Satisfies

Once you start your smoking-cessation plan, as you gradually reduce your number of cigarettes daily while simultaneously replacing smoking rituals with new oral, hand, and body activities, here's how to "pig out" with impunity (within reason) and not get fat: serve the "defatted calf," literally. Yes, there *is* a popular brand of virtually fat-free roast beef in the deli section of your local food market. You'll also

find fat-free wieners, bologna, and other cold cuts. Fat-free cheeses are available, as well as virtually fat-free bacon and egg substitutes (or, you can use regular eggs, spray your pan with a calorie-free cooking oil, and "fry" the egg whites). Fresh fruit and veggies, skinless chicken and turkey, fish, seafood, low-fat and fat-free breads and pastas abound. Tasty saccharine-free sugar substitutes are readily available as are many very low-fat and fat-free desserts. There are lots of choices.

Read the labels, ignoring percentages of fat while noting *the number of grams of fat* listed per serving re: processed foods. The following formula will make it easy for you: each gram of fat contains 9 calories. If a product label states its content of fat is, for example, "only 3 grams of fat" per serving and the total number of calories per serving are listed as 60, then multiply 3×9 and you can easily see that almost one-half (about 27 calories) of the 60-calorie content of the product's suggested serving is derived from fat! Avoid that fat-laden product and move on to fat-free and lower-fat versions of same.

Prominent health organizations, including the American Heart Association and the American Cancer Society, recommend that your fat intake amount to no more than 30 percent of your daily calorie consumption. The Pritikin program and other well-known nutritional health authorities have recommended taking your daily fat consumption down to between 5 and 10 percent. Perhaps a reasonable middle ground would be 20 percent. *Consult your doctor* for advice concerning your daily fat intake. You generally can't go wrong with plenty of fresh vegetables, fruits, beans/legumes, high-fiber/low-fat foods, fish, seafood, and turkey and chicken (minus the fatty skin, and baked, not fried).

Remember, in earlier chapters I've tried to put a fine point to the fact that "it's not nice to try to screw mother nature," meaning you should "masturbate your inner child": If you deprive your primitive self, your primitive self will get even. Reasonable indulgence in fat-

free and low-fat versions of creamy/crunchy/sweet/spicy treats brings necessary human satisfaction.

A helpful hint: Drink two liters of water every day. People often think they are hungry when, in reality, they are thirsty—stay hydrated.

Smart Fitness without Pain

Here's how to get fit, stay fit, and not be nauseating about it: Don't remain stationary; you're not a "still life." Exercise entails movement of the body by one's own power. This movement need not be oppressive, obsessive, or excessive. *Consult your doctor* regarding a safe, sane exercise/fitness plan for your individual situation.

Personally, I prefer what studies have shown to help keep folks of all ages generally in good shape: moderate *daily* exercise. Aerobics—physical conditioning involving exercises such as walking, running, bicycling, swimming, or calisthenics—temporarily increases respiration and heart rate and reduces your risk of stroke, heart attack, cancer, obesity, and diabetes. You experience increased endurance and an increased sense of accomplishment and well-being.

At this writing, I'm fifty-six years of age and I do daily exercise (unless I'm temporarily "under the weather" with a cold or flu). My target area is the solar plexus, or gut. I do stomach crunches, push-ups, pull-ups, and some walking/running. My regular regimen takes approximately twenty minutes. Like many men and women, my initial experiences with exercise were competitive conditioning programs in public school. I perceived exercise—as, I suspect, many others did—as punishment, a disciplinary tactic.

It's certainly not surprising that many folks associate exercising with pain and boredom. We sometimes feel overworked and overwhelmed, we give up and feel a sense of failure, resentment, dread, and resistance toward oppressive exercise. Leave that "crap" behind you, where it belongs, and plan your own personal moderate fitness approach with your doctor's help, if possible. Perhaps you will prefer to breathe deeply and exercise your major muscles rhythmically, continuously, to music in the privacy of your own place. Perhaps you'll prefer the supportive atmosphere of a trendy gym.

I keep an accurate body-weight scale in my bedroom, and I climb onto it each morning, realizing realistically that each individual's weight can fluctuate a bit from day to day. I maintain a healthy weight (160 pounds) for my bone structure (medium) and my height of 5'10".

Without time-consuming oppressive pain-and-gain exercises from the school of "terminal perkiness," you'll discover a world of "smart fitness" that is actually fun.

Sense-Memory Empowerment

Momentarily revisiting the sense-memory teachings of the dead-as-a-doornail dramatist Constantin Stanislavski, it's important to note that, unlike other species, we've got *imagination* going for us. We can use imagination to our advantage, to get us *unhooked* from nicotine and to *keep* us *unhooked* from nicotine. Continue your sense-memory mirror work and try "superimposing" these imaginative conceptions over what I call the occasional "Pavlovian pull." (You may recall the Nobel Prize-winning Russian physiologist, Ivan Petrovich Pavlov, who proved his theory of the conditioned response as a basic model of mental activity by regularly ringing a bell while feeding his dogs. He found that eventually the sound of the bell alone, even in the absence of food, caused the dogs to salivate; the dogs had become conditioned to associate the sound of the bell with food.)

When struck by your own "Pavlovian pull," that is, your momentary pleasurable smoking associations, in addition to impactful declarations of self-truth regarding the *real* consequences of smoking, why not try some creative imagery as well? For example, when you get a "Bette Davis flashback" or a "to-hell-with-it-all-it-ain't-that-bad-anyway-and-I-need-a-cigarette-get-out-of-my-way" thinking/feeling/smoking association distortion in your perception, try *mentally dumping* your choice of human, dog, or bull feces onto your Pavlovian "cigarette scene." Allow yourself to see this smelly substance glopping, dripping off bejeweled hands and onto packs of cigarettes, smearing across mouths, stifling hollow peals of laughter, etc. Get the picture? In fact, use *any* mental picture that, for you, breaks the momentary "B.S. thought" that cigarettes are "really OK," or "OK or not, I'll have one, now!"

Creating Your Own Antismoking Ads

You have *every right*, having been addicted for years to the products pushed by those "tobacco bastards" and their pervasive, grossly misleading ads—associating cigarette smoking with robust health, human sexuality, beauty, wealth, fame, etc.—to create your own *aggressive* ad campaign in your head and gut! When you see billboards or print ads for cigarettes, try adding your own (preferably scandalous) captions to the mouths of macho and glamorous smokers shown therein. How about, in a nicotine-country scene, one smoker cowpoke to another: "Hey, sh-thead, I'm dying of lung cancer!" The other smoker cowboy's reply might be, "Shut the hell up! Can't you see I'm having a heart attack?" Or in a back-to-nature outdoors setting, a beautiful smoker maiden might utter to her smoker boyfriend, "Don't worry about me getting pregnant; I took precautions to avoid having a possible 'problem pregnancy'!" Her boyfriend, standing near the humongous waterfall, might reply, "You don't have to worry. What you felt in the dark was a dildo; I'm impotent!"

Another fun-time nicotine-addiction recovery activity is to focus in on the small Surgeon General's warning box, relegated (in small type) to the bottom of cigarette print ads, and read the copy aloud, for example: "Smoking causes lung cancer, heart disease, emphysema, and may complicate pregnancy." This helps negate the powerful positive associations shown in cigarette ads.

Smokeless Expectations

Smoker to smoker . . . I've felt more in touch with life since I stopped smoking. My spirit of adventure isn't stifled or delayed. My movements are more fluid; I feel more "in the moment" of life without mandatory cigarette breaks. There is, after all, lots of stuff to do, think about, and feel, without nicotine impairment.

Once we escape from nicotine country, we have the opportunity, in the full fresh air, to rediscover unblunted joy. We can look deep into our mirrors, smoke-free, and repeat positive impactful affirmations to ourselves:

- My teeth are whiter, my breath is fresher, my mind is clear of carcinogens.
- My lungs are pinker, my food tastes better, my sense of smell is back.
- My stamina has increased, and I feel more like participating exuberantly in my clear reality.

Before you begin your smoking-cessation plan, allow me to say that I've *never* regretted my escape from nicotine country. As I continue to "stay real" about my arrested addiction to cigarettes, I revel in freedom from slavery. My life, without cigarettes, has become more comfortable. Even in the face of inevitable real-life challenges, I am clear-headed, less depressed.

You, dear smoker, may be a woman or a man, younger or older than yours truly. You're poised at the beginning of a new era for yourself. Perhaps you're concerned that you may "screw it all up." If you relapse, simply start afresh. If you like the concept of a self-help support-group approach, read chapter 6 for suggestions about how to start such a group—a great recovery activity for some—or refer to "References/Resources" in the back of this book for support systems and other groups already in existence.

My dear smoker, the rituals we've all partaken in over the years—sharing "special cigarette moments" with each other—contain human warmth, a sense of belonging, and poisonous B.S. Simply extract the good stuff: When approaching another human being, "break the ice" by acknowledging the person's existence with a simple "hello." Get all "toasty" during a friendly conversation, while fiddling, perhaps, with a wrapper from a piece of sugarless gum you've just offered your new potential compadre, instead of blowing smoke into her face or turning aside repeatedly to cough.

The comfortable "taper" method you'll be using to gradually escape from nicotine country while the "smoking forces" are sleeping, so to speak, allows you to saddle up, mount, and calmly ride out on the horse you rode in on. As dawn breaks, that is to say, when you've "tapered" to the point of having smoked your final cigarette, the grip of nicotine in your system has dwindled, diminished into the distance. And, as the sun brings a new day, your successful escape from nicotine country is complete, as you continue on, at full gallop, into the sunset. But, as you're well aware, movie scenarios end; life, however, goes on, sunset to sunset.

Riding without stumbling may seem like "second nature" to you, but it does require your relaxed attention (*not* tension). To avoid being "caught off guard," drugged and dragged back into the depths of nicotine country, *all* you have to do is to stay real about the fact that you *cannot* "*light up*" (a cigarette, that is). You can light up in numerous other ways, *real* ways, rather than experiencing your existence as a servant to cigarettes.

Smokin' Dreams!

I've had "smoking dreams" after I stopped smoking cigarettes, just as I had "drinking dreams" after I stopped drinking alcoholic beverages, many years before. And, having experienced drinking dreams, I knew what to expect. The substance-use dream seems real and, upon awakening (especially from a deep sleep), I felt (as have countless others who've shared this phenomenon with me) momentarily startled. "Oh no, I've smoked again. I'm hooked again," I thought. Although, more precisely, I should characterize this event as a split-moment. Why? Because for one-half of a moment I felt startled (bad) and then almost instantaneously (the second half of the moment) I felt enormous relief and joy, basking in my *genuine* reality: "Whew! I'm OK. I didn't smoke. It was only a dream!"

People, Places, Things

What about smoking friends, smoking places, smoking-related activities? Do we have to give 'em up? I didn't. Some of the world's most fascinating people are addicted to cigarettes. Some of the world's most interesting places are loaded with smokers. As for "smoking-related" activities, let's get real and agree that, for a smoker, just about any person, place, or thing can be "smoking-related."

Simple modifications are in order, and virtually all smokers respect them: State your case honestly, while respecting the rights of others. Say that you can't tolerate smoke in a closed space and virtually all smokers will meet you halfway. Virtually any situation can be worked out for both nonsmoker and smoker alike. And in your new freedom from cigarettes, don't, please don't, become a self-righteous asshole!

All best wishes to you as you continue in preparation for your gradual smoking-cessation plan. Go on to chapter 6.

Just Do It
(with a Little Help from Your Friends)

Smokers are all kinds of people, all kinds of people are smokers. Before my memory began, the Americas produced bountiful tobacco crops. Explorers—Chris Columbus included—took this native American product back to Europe.

Later, early American tobacco interests—colonial precursors, perhaps, to cigarette-company CEOs—were pissed at Britain for "taxation without representation" and helped finance the American Revolutionary War. Since then, until relatively recently, we, for a variety of reasons, have not placed the consequences of tobacco use in a harsh light. We've been naïve, I suppose, but we've been busy, too—no time (or funds) to invest in research about a profitable product that offers folks coming-of-age adult fun that only finger-wagging prudes have heretofore disdained.

49

Notice, however, that not even "tobacco interests" have ever had the moxie to suggest "smoking in moderation." To do so would be tantamount to an admission that this stuff is *mucho addictive* and that "smoking in moderation" is virtually impossible for most folks indigenous to this planet. Of course, everyone knows that chewing tobacco and using snuff are basically passé (and gross), but what about pipes? Cigars?

I have a close friend who can "take it or leave it" with cigars. After all, he doesn't inhale. He eventually shared, however, that when it comes right down to it, he'd rather take it than leave it. He needs his nicotine.

Although movie icons blow smoke rings of stardust, you, too, can "get real" about your addiction. Carcinogenic whirls of smoke create, perhaps, a naughty grown-up-so-the-fuck-whatness obscuring one's bottom-line cellular need agenda.

How much have you gone through to get your nicotine fix? Ever "bum" a cigarette? Drive to a late-night minimart in the wee hours for a pack of smokes? Extract yourself from an "oppressive" smoke-free environment ASAP for a drag? Repeatedly endure inclement weather, fumbling for a light? You might find a self-empowerment support group that addresses tobacco-addiction issues helpful.

Here's what you can do. Attend an already-existing support group (see the back of this book for listings) or start one. We can launch free, grassroots, autonomous, self-empowerment support groups right here, right now. As mentioned earlier, I started such groups primarily for alcoholics and drug addicts some years ago, back in 1985 to be precise. You can find out more about SOS (Save Our Selves) groups in the back of this book.

I now offer *this* proposal: groups *specifically* for people who want to stop tobacco use. Call them "Escape from Nicotine Country" groups. This chapter contains all you need to begin and maintain such a group in your own home or local community center.

Your group could consist of yourself and only one other person. The **OBJECTIVE** is the same, whatever the size of your new group: to offer a supportive self-help group forum for anyone who has a desire to achieve and maintain freedom from cigarettes and all other tobacco products.

Introduction to ENC Groups

You're most welcome to check out www.unhooked.com, which contains a "stop smoking" section; however, its cyberspace members who stay in supportive contact with each other, via e-mail, are *alcoholics and addicts who also want to stop smoking.* "Escape from Nicotine Country" groups, conversely, are nicotine-addiction specific, that is, these groups are open to *anyone* who desires freedom from tobacco products.

Borrowing from my experience with SOS meetings, I offer the following information in a question-and-answer presentation:

Q: What method of smoking cessation will individual members of the group use?

A: "Escape from Nicotine Country" groups encourage the use of *any* smoking- (or tobacco-use-) cessation method that works for the individual. Individual group members are free to utilize any of the smoking-cessation taper plans offered in this book; however, members are by no means limited to this approach. They may have decided to stop smoking "cold turkey," that is to say, at once, on a preset date of their own choice. Individual members may be involved in another program, following the advice of their family physician, for example.

Q: What, then, will be the meeting FORMAT?

A: The following nicotine-addiction-specific format is a modified version of a successful self-help support group format that I developed well over a decade ago:

Suggested Format

Welcome to the "Escape from Nicotine Country" group's regular _____-night meeting. My name is _____. I have been asked to lead tonight's meeting.

The OBJECTIVE of this meeting is to offer a supportive forum for anyone who has a desire to achieve and maintain freedom from cigarettes and all other tobacco products. We respect diversity and encourage rational thinking as well as the expression of feelings. We each take responsibility for our individual recovery. This is an autonomous, nonprofessional, self-empowerment support group. At this meeting we will share our experiences, understandings, thoughts, and feelings.

We encourage the use of *any* smoking-cessation METHOD that works for you. Consult your doctor before beginning any smoking-cessation plan.

Individual group members are free to utilize any of the smoking-cessation taper plans offered in the book *Escape from Nicotine Country*; however, you are by no means limited to this approach. You may have decided to stop smoking "cold turkey," that is to say, at once, on a preset date of your own choice. You may be involved in another program, following the advice of your family physician, for example. We celebrate and applaud recovery from tobacco addiction, whatever your choice of method.

The "cycle of nicotine addiction" contains three debilitating elements: *chemical need* (at the physiological-cellular level), *learned habit* (chronic behaviors and associations), and *denial* of both need and habit.

The cycle of nicotine addiction can be successfully replaced by another cycle: the "cycle of recovery." This cycle contains three essential elements: *acknowledgment* of your addiction to nicotine, *acceptance* of your addiction, and *prioritization* of recovery procedures to replace the addiction. This group respects all approaches to recovery from nicotine addiction.

ANNOUNCEMENTS: Ask for announcements from group members. Announce new literature, meeting schedules, etc. Indicate if nonalcoholic beverages or other refreshments are available. Let the group know the meeting length (usually one hour is typical) and if there will be a break (usually five to ten minutes) during the course of the meeting. Inform the group of the time and place of your next meeting.

ANNIVERSARIES: We celebrate various lengths of freedom from nicotine addiction in these meetings. Is there anyone here with thirty days of continuous freedom from nicotine addiction? Sixty days? Three months? Six months? Nine months? Is there anyone celebrating a yearly anniversary this week? Congratulations, all! (Applause.)

READING: Tonight I have asked _____ to read our suggested group guidelines:

- To break the cycle of denial and achieve freedom from nicotine addiction, we "get real" and acknowledge the addiction as a separate issue from everything else.
- We "stay real" about this issue by reaffirming daily and accepting without reservation that we cannot use tobacco with impunity, that is, *we cannot get away with it.*
- Since smoking or using tobacco is not an option for us, we take whatever steps are necessary to keep our addiction arrested for life.
- A quality of life, "the good life," can be achieved. Of course, life is also filled with uncertainties, but we do not smoke or use tobacco, no matter what.

- We share in confidence with each other our thoughts and feelings as individuals in recovery from addiction to tobacco.
- We are each individually responsible for our lives and our recovery, achieving and maintaining freedom from smoking and using tobacco.

INTRODUCTIONS: Again, I'm _____. Now, starting with the person on my left, let's introduce ourselves.

OPENING: This meeting is now open. We ask that you try to keep your sharing to a reasonable length of time so that everyone can participate.

CLOSING: This group is self-supporting. We have no dues or fees. If you can make some contribution, we will use it to help defray the cost of rent, refreshments, and other expenses. (Pass the basket.) Thanks for coming and please come back. Let's close by giving ourselves a hand for being here to support and celebrate each other's recovery.

Q: What constitutes the "heart" of a meeting? What do we talk about? What's the structure of the "sharing segment"?

A: Simple, straightforward, human, common-cause, tobacco-addiction-specific sharing of thoughts and feelings in an effort to achieve and maintain individual freedom from addiction, and to support one another in that process, is the "heart" of a meeting.

The individual meeting leader (or secretary or chair) can introduce a topic for discussion to "get the ball rolling." Here are some sample topics:*

---

*Modified and reprinted, by permission, from *Sobriety Handbook: The SOS Way* (Oakland, Calif.: LifeRing Press, 1997), p. 87.

Accepting things I can't change

Addictive thinking

Anger

Awareness of my own self and feelings

Blame

Change

Changes we can make in our behavior

Changing my environment

Control

Death

Denial

Dependence

Discussing portions of Jim's book *Escape from Nicotine Country*

Falling back into old patterns

Fear

Feelings

Getting real

Grieving

Guilt

Happiness

Honesty

Joy

Little lies

Meetings as a lifeline

My smoking-cessation plan

My story that brought me here

Pain

Progress in recovery

Recovery

Relapse

Relationships

Responsibility

Scary things

Serendipity

Shame

Stress

Taking responsibility

Thoughts and words

Triggers and cravings

Trust

Values

What brought me to recovery

What I am thankful for

What kind of smoker am I?

What this meeting means to me

Your meeting discussion/sharing period could proceed with no particular topic, per se, and general discussion/sharing of thoughts and feelings *related to recovery from nicotine addiction* can evolve into a wonderfully supportive evening. You could choose to call on each member, one by one, to share. You could, after throwing the meeting open with an announced topic (or no topic in particular) remain silent as members elect to share or not to share, moving at their own pace.

You could build in a "sharing safety component," immediately before opening the meeting to discussion/sharing, by stating something like this: "It is assumed that you do *not* want feedback after your individual "share" *unless* you specifically request it.

Q: What are the "underpinnings" of the group meeting, if any?

A: The following are offered as your group's general principles:

All those who have a desire to achieve and maintain freedom from cigarettes and other tobacco products are welcome as members in our group. We have no hidden agenda. We are not a spin-off of any other group or program. We seek only to promote recovery among those who are addicted to tobacco. As a group, we have no opinion on outside matters and do not wish to become entangled in outside controversy.

Although recovery is an individual responsibility, life does not have to be faced alone. The support of others is a vital adjunct to recovery. In our group, members share experiences, insights, information, strength, and encouragement in friendly, honest, and supportive group meetings.

To avoid unnecessary entanglement, our group is self-supporting through contributions from its members, and refuses outside support.

Our group does not limit its outlook to one area of knowledge or method of recovery. We encourage the use of *any* smoking- (or tobacco use-) cessation method that works for the individual.

Q: What about anonymity? Does that matter nowadays in a nicotine-specific addiction-arrest support group?

A: Although there is far less stigma attached to smoking and using other tobacco products than there is to other drug use, nicotine addiction is a serious matter. Therefore, it is prudent to assume group members prefer a "first name only" basis, unless they state otherwise, i.e., optional anonymity makes good sense.

Q: What about relapse? How should that be handled?

A: Relapse can occur in the recovery process. Your group is a *support* group; therefore members who experience relapse during their recovery process should be heartily *encouraged* to continue their recovery process in the group.

Q: How long should one typically attend our group meetings? How long should our group continue to exist?

A: Individual members attend as long as they deem appropriate for their needs. They may still wish to support the group by continuing to attend, even after they feel secure in their own recovery. Groups tend to continue to exist as long as members value their existence.

Q: How does one go about setting up a new group? What are the particulars? How are leadership roles defined?

A: Over a decade ago, after I founded the Save Our Selves movement, we SOS members put together a little yellow booklet entitled *SOS Group Leader's Guidebook*. In 1997, some members crafted an updated and expanded version of that early effort, entitled *Sobriety Handbook: The SOS Way*. What follows are excerpts from that more recent work,* modified for use in forming and maintaining nicotine-addiction-specific groups.

The Care and Feeding of Your Group

If a group is to work well for its members as a place to build their recovery, careful attention must be paid to the way it is set up and

*Modified and reprinted, by permission, from *Sobriety Handbook: The SOS Way* (Oakland, Calif.: LifeRing Press, 1997), pp. 59–77, 88–90.

operated. Leadership roles, meeting format, and finances are three points that require particular attention. You have complete autonomy in how you structure your group, as long as you adhere to our general principles, outlined earlier. This section contains some ideas and examples drawn from earlier recovery groups, which you can use for suggestion and inspiration.

[A] Leadership

There was a heavy rain at a Friday-night meeting, and the meeting secretary, who traveled by bicycle, was definitely going to be late. He had the only copy of the opening statement with him. No matter; at a few minutes after the hour, the members collectively pieced the opening statement together from memory, and the meeting began. Nearly everyone present was a leader, and any one of them could have opened, led, and closed the meeting. The more there are who can do this, the stronger the group. A group in which only one or two can lead is fragile, weak.

Typically, the group defines two or more leadership roles that rotate among the members. The most essential roles are those of secretary and of treasurer.

The **secretary** (also often called convenor) would typically include in his or her job description the following: arrive a few minutes early to open up, turn on the lights, arrange the room, set up the literature, bring the opening statement and the sign-up sheet, read or get someone to read the opening statement, keep the discussion on the foundations (if necessary), deal with problem situations as required, pass around and collect the sign-up sheet (if one is used), keep an eye on the clock, and bring the meeting to a close.

Some meeting secretaries do more, for example, maintaining the voicemail or message machine for the group's contact telephone number, if applicable, etc. Your group may wish to divide these responsibilities among several members.

The **treasurer** is necessary because the organization has expenses and needs to collect funds. Most meeting sites charge rent. Flyers, literature, telephone lines, phonebook listings, and other goods and services the group deems essential must all be supported out of group funds.

Elect as treasurer someone who is a regular with the group, who is financially stable, and whose home address is known to group members. The treasurer typically keeps a basket, a book, and the funds. The treasurer passes the basket; a good time is when everyone has arrived at the meeting who is expected to arrive. At the end of the meeting the treasurer tallies the contents, and records the amount in the book. It is a good idea also to record the amount on the meeting sign-up sheet, if used, as a backup. The treasurer pays the meeting rent and whatever other expenditures the meeting has decided, and makes a financial report to the group. The treasurer's job also should rotate as much as is practical.

You may also want to have:

- a librarian, responsible for getting and distributing relevant books, pamphlets, flyers, meeting schedules, and other material, and perhaps for leading group discussion based on reading material
- a publicity person, responsible for outreach, placing ads, etc.
- a refreshment coordinator
- a new member secretary, responsible for following up with new members to make sure their questions are answered and their concerns addressed

Leadership is a necessary service to the group. People who have performed these services testify that doing so helps their recovery.

Doing service work strengthens their recovery identity, helps them to feel good about recovery, and motivates them to do more. The opportunity to render leadership services needs to be shared as widely as possible among the regular group participants.

Leadership can also have its negative side. Leaders may come to feel, after a time, that they are better, wiser, stronger, or smarter than others, and may begin to pose as gurus, amateur therapists, or authorities over the members. That kind of "leadership" is a departure from the self-help foundation of your group. Regular rotation of leadership positions helps to keep this kind of corruption from developing.

Elections to leadership in ongoing meetings are usually by consensus. Elections will not be very useful if they are held by surprise or without preparation, if two camps form, if less than the full membership is present, or if the voting is secret. Elections are most useful if they are announced in advance, if volunteers are sought or nominated in advance, if there is already consensus, and if the full membership of the meeting is there to vote by a simple show of hands with the candidates present. There are no speeches. Usually elections are simple, trouble-free affairs that occupy at most a few minutes of the meeting's time.

[B] Opening Statement

The opening statement is a useful ritual that signals the formal beginning of the meeting. It informs newcomers and reminds regular members of the basic purpose of the group. It outlines the format and ground rules of the meeting. It gets the ball rolling. Usually the meeting secretary reads the statement or asks for a volunteer to read it.

Each group is free to compose its own opening statement, provided the contents are consistent with the general principles, outlined earlier. Drafting or revising an opening statement might be a good process for the members of a new group to go through as part of their self-help activity.

Directly after the reading of the opening statement, many meetings allow for introductions, especially of newcomers. Newcomers may be invited to state their first names and to say a few words about themselves. Then everyone in the meeting will do likewise in response.

Announcements and time for special concerns usually follow directly after introductions. Announcements include other meetings or social events, and business items. Members will sometimes announce here that they plan to be absent at the next meeting for vacation or for some other reason. "Special concerns" is a broad category that allows members to put on the meeting's agenda important events in their lives during the past week. Members here share such events as recovery anniversaries, relapses, job losses or promotions, graduations, marriages, births, deaths, injuries, and the like. In some cases, the concern turns into the main topic of the meeting; in others, it passes without comment.

After announcements and special concerns comes the main part of the meeting. How this is handled varies from group to group. Some groups simply go to open discussion with no definite theme. Others use the "chair" system with a defined topic, or focus the discussion on selected readings passed out in advance. Some allow crosstalk during the whole meeting; others only in part of the meeting, or not at all. Below are some of the points you may want to consider when deciding which format to use.

[C] Sharing and Crosstalk

"Sharing" has a very definite meaning in self-help groups. It means that the person recounts his or her experience and thoughts, without expecting response or comment of any sort. Sharing is an exclusively one-way form of communication. It is a monologue. In technical terms, it is a half-duplex connection. The person talks, everybody else listens. Then the next person talks, and everybody else listens. Then the next. At no point is anyone's "share" an answer or other direct response to anyone else's. Each share stands entirely on its own, complete and sufficient unto itself.

"Crosstalk" means two-way communication, dialogue, a full-duplex connection. In crosstalk, a person expects a response and may respond in turn, creating a conversation. A third may join in, and more, until everybody is chattering away like birds in spring.

Although crosstalk feels more natural and may appear to be more therapeutic, many contend that the real work in self-help groups is done during sharing time. The "no response" rule of sharing time protects the speakers from having their statements judged, criticized, ridiculed, or otherwise attacked. This in turn promotes the fullest possible openness and honesty, qualities that are essential to self-change. When sharing is at its best, speakers will find themselves saying things they did not consciously plan, which came out of their mouths from some inner concern of which they were unaware. These can be powerful moments of self-revelation and self-acceptance. These times, when the self-help process is visibly at work, are precious, awesome moments in a group's life.

Crosstalk needs to be handled with great care, respect, and humor. We in recovery have typically gone through pain, guilt, shame, and a mess of other feelings. We may be raw, edgy, timid, depressed, or a combination of all the above. So, rudeness, sarcasm, and thoughtlessness are not appreciated; preaching and unasked advice will quickly make enemies; and even ordinary, innocent curiosity may deeply threaten or offend someone. The most valued qualities in crosstalk are kindness, sincerity, tact, and above all, humor. The member who can make the group laugh is always a valued crosstalk participant.

Sharing and crosstalk both have their place. Many meetings allot three-fourths of the main meeting time to sharing, one-fourth to crosstalk. What you do in your meeting is up to you.

[D] Chair and Topic

During the main part of your meeting, discussion may be completely random, or you may try to organize it around a topic. If you use the topic system, you will want a person to introduce the topic and get the talk rolling. That person is usually called a chairperson, or just "chair," but may be called "speaker" or something else. Since chairs are best designated in advance, you will also need a sign-up list, and the secretary (or someone else) will need to circulate this and make sure that a volunteer for the next meeting has come forward. You will need a fall-back procedure for those weeks when the designated chair is unexpectedly absent. Some groups make this their "round-robin" night when everyone talks in turn about their personal recovery program.

The chair's duty is to select a topic and introduce it. No special qualification or length of recovery is required to be chair. It is an excellent task for persons early in recovery. Selecting a topic may occupy the chairperson's mind with recovery thoughts daily or hourly for the week before the meeting, which is very therapeutic. Introducing the topic with a few minutes' talk is a good way to learn the skill of sharing. The chair may also conduct the meeting during sharing time, taking over temporarily from the secretary, and thus can practice meeting leadership skills, with the secretary available as a backup.

The chair-and-topic system is meant to rotate the chair each week and give everyone a turn at setting the topic. In this way, all participants have their concern aired by the whole meeting periodically, ensuring that meetings don't become monopolized by the interests of one or a handful of talkative individuals.

If you use the chair-and-topic system, why not keep a record of the topic? Make a space on the sign-up sheet for it. After a while you'll have a treasure trove of topics to consult, which can help chairpersons who are searching for one topic, and can also call up memories of outstanding meetings for you.

The chair-and-topic system is not meant to be a rigid mold. If you have nothing to share on the evening's topic, but have something entirely different on your mind, by all means share that. It often takes just a little stretching, and can be a source of general merriment, to "relate" your concern to the topic, no matter how improbably.

[E] Sign-up Sheet

Many, but not all, groups make use of a sign-up sheet. A sample sign-up sheet is given at the end of this chapter. Signing the sheet and giving your phone number is always optional, and the general practice is to use first names and last initials only. The sheet has several purposes. By signing and putting your telephone number on the list, you give permission to other members to call you if they need help. The secretary can use the sign-up sheet as a record of meeting attendance over time. The sheet also helps the members get to know each other's names, and serves as a way of affirming their recovery psychologically by "signing in" to the meeting. The secretary circulates, collects, and preserves the sign-up sheets.

[F] Closing

Our meetings end without any sort of ceremony. The secretary merely seizes on the appropriate moment to state that it's time to go. A happy ceremony that some groups practice is to give each other, at the end, a round of applause for one another's recovery.

Some groups make it a custom to go out for refreshments after the meeting. This promotes friendship among the members and gives the meeting a stronger sense of community. This is desirable, since that is essentially what the group is: a self-help community.

How to Start Your Group

Even with no help and limited resources, starting a group is not difficult. The only true requirement for starting a group is the honest desire to do so and the energy to make that desire real. You can set up a time and place to meet, publicize that information, and then be there. If only one other person shows up, you can have a meeting.

[1] Starting Up

The Meeting Place

You will need to settle on a place to meet. You could start a group in your home. If your community is very small or there is no way that you can do otherwise, go ahead. But most people will find a public meeting place is preferable. Additionally, if you try to have meetings in a member's home or in any other place owned or controlled by a member, you may encounter proprietary problems. If that is all you have at the beginning, you may have to make do with it. But consider rental of a neutral place as soon as possible.

A meeting place can be just about anywhere, but it is more likely that you will attract others to the meeting if it is held in a relatively convenient, comfortable, and safe place. Many places recommend themselves as meeting places for a group meeting. Places that may have meeting spaces available include libraries, schools, colleges and universities, hospitals, community parks and recreation centers, banks, public utilities, union halls, and even churches, as long as the separation of your group and the church is clear.

Choose according to your size and financial ability. Whatever you do, tell the owner ahead of time the purpose of your group. Do all you can to avoid any possible future misunderstanding that might surprise anyone and cause disruption to your meeting.

You should base your choice on your best judgment as to the needs of your proposed group. If funds are scarce, and no doubt they will be, suggest to your potential landlord a payment of a percentage of your meeting's collection. Even if a meeting place is offered to you at no charge, a small payment toward electricity and other expenses is always appreciated. By doing this, you maintain group autonomy, avoid possible conflicts, and enhance group esteem.

The Meeting Time and Length

Once you have a place to meet, the next step is to determine when you meet and for how long. Again, the choice is entirely up to those in your group. Having a meeting one evening a week is the usual pattern. You may have to experiment to find which day and time are best. There are successful meetings at breakfast time, lunch, mid-afternoon, and evening.

Pick what works for you. Meetings traditionally last from an hour to an hour and a half. Again, try what you think will work, and change it later if you need to. Whatever you finally decide upon, try to be consistent. This last point is important. Once you establish a meeting time and place, be there, rain or shine.

Finding Allies

Starting a group and attending meetings with regularity is an active and strong affirmation of your recovery. The benefits derived from meeting attendance are many: camaraderie, sharing of experience, a sense of belonging, to name but a few. But first and foremost is the fact that you have made a strong behavioral statement for you and your recovery.

The task of establishing a group by yourself can be daunting. You can lighten that burden and give your group a head start by finding an ally. An ally is another person who shares your commitment to recovery and is as willing as you to devote some time and energy to getting the group going.

Finding yourself an ally prior to starting a group has the added benefit of allowing you to find out how receptive your area is to having a new group meeting. Additionally, having an ally will enable you to share the legwork necessary to getting your group off the ground. And, of course, come meeting time, you won't be sitting there alone. Your group will already have at least two members.

[2] Promotion

You have to let people know where you are and what you are doing. Be ready to invest some time, energy, and perhaps a little money. You can try these strategies:

- Mail press releases to local radio stations. Address them to the Program Director or Public Service Director for each station. See sample press release at the end of the chapter.
- Mail press releases to local newspapers, daily and weekly. Address them to the Editorial Department. If you know that a

paper has a community calendar, mail a press release to that department for a possible listing.

- Mail press releases and bulletin-board announcements to any local cable television companies in your community. Many cable companies will run this kind of announcement on the local access channel on a continuing basis.

- Make extensive use of bulletin boards in laundromats, food markets, gyms, hospitals, schools, colleges, senior-citizen centers, neighborhood centers, etc. See the sample flyer in the appendix.

- Contact local "throw-away" free papers. Some of these may run regular meeting announcement listings in their "ongoing groups" section at no charge. Find out what their requirements are and make use of these free listings.

- Print business cards with your name and phone number, along with the time, day, and location of your meeting. Place these cards anywhere that you think interested people may find them.

The suggestions here are very basic in nature, and you will probably think of other good ways to reach those who need your group. As your group develops, you will have help in getting the word out. It will, no doubt, take a while before you see meaningful results. Stick with it and try to be patient—it is important not to let yourself become overwhelmed.

Sample Meeting Sign-up Sheet

(City), (Day of the Week) Meeting
(Location) Optional Sign-up Sheet
Date _____

NAME	PHONE	NAME	PHONE
_____	_____	_____	_____
_____	_____	_____	_____
_____	_____	_____	_____
_____	_____	_____	_____
_____	_____	_____	_____
_____	_____	_____	_____
_____	_____	_____	_____
_____	_____	_____	_____
_____	_____	_____	_____
_____	_____	_____	_____

Mtg Secy: _____ Treas: _____
Chair: _____ Chair Next Week: _____
Topic: _____
$ Donated: _____

BOOKS BORROWED   BORROWER

_____   _____
_____   _____
_____   _____
_____   _____

Sample New-Meeting Flyer

Had Enough?

There is a new free self-help support group for smokers who want to quit in the (City) area!

"Escape from Nicotine Country"
Stop-Smoking Group to Start

The "Escape from Nicotine Country" group, based on addiction specialist James Christopher's book of the same name, *suggests* a "taper" (gradual-reduction) approach to stop smoking, but welcomes all smoking-cessation approaches as equally valid. Members meet for mutual support regarding their individual stop-smoking plans.

Every (Day of Week)
(Time), (Room), (Building)
(Street Address, City, ZIP)
(Directions, if necessary)

For more information about the new meeting, contact (local contact person) at (local telephone number).

Sample Press Release

FOR IMMEDIATE RELEASE

"Escape from Nicotine Country"
Stop-Smoking Group to Start

A free support group for smokers who want to stop is coming soon. Meetings will be held every (day of week) night, beginning (day of month), (year), at (time) P.M. in (room) of (building) on (street address), in the (neighborhood) area of (town).

The new "Escape from Nicotine Country" group, based on addiction specialist James Christopher's book of the same name, *suggests* a "taper" (gradual-reduction) approach to stop smoking, but welcomes all smoking-cessation approaches as equally valid. Members meet for mutual support regarding their individual stop-smoking plans.

For further information about the new meeting, contact (name of local contact person) at (local telephone number).

—30—

- -

How's your group?

After you get started . . . write and let us know how your group is doing. I look forward to hearing from you.

Jim Christopher
ENC Groups
PO Box 9522
Marina del Rey CA 90295

Let's Get Started!

Even if you are reading this book out of curiosity with, perhaps, only a "half-assed" interest in stopping smoking, that's OK. That's a beginning. However, I can't offer you more than the *potential* of a smoke-free life, with, I might add, lots of support from people just like you who've already achieved a smoke-free life. And you can't escape to a smoke-free life unless you begin.

Important note: Prior to beginning any smoking-cessation program, it is advisable to go over it with your doctor. Your physician can be a valuable ally in your efforts.

The gradual smoking-cessation segment of this book is designed to accommodate those who smoke from one pack to three packs of cigarettes per day. Simply determine the number of cigarettes realistically appropriate for your "DAY 1" based upon what you typically smoke in a 24-hour period. Choose A, B, or C and begin. If you determine that another number is your true count, simply stop at that point in one of the three plans.

Plan A   75

Three-Packs-per-Day Addiction Gradual-Cessation Smoking Log

Plan B   107

Two-Packs-per-Day Addiction Gradual-Cessation Smoking Log

Plan C   129

One-Pack-per-Day Addiction Gradual-Cessation Smoking Log

For instance, if you typically smoke one and a half packs per day, choose Plan B (40 cigarettes), and stop at "DAY 30," *writing in your true count* in the *alternate count* space provided for each day. This option is available for all three plans.

If you typically smoke *more* than three packs of cigarettes (60 cigarettes) per day, simply begin your program on an additional sheet of paper and continue into the log in this book, choosing Plan A.

Plan A
Three-Packs-Per-Day Addiction:
Gradual-Cessation Smoking Log

DAY 1 or DAY ___

I typically smoke three packs of cigarettes in a 24-hour period. My allotment for today is a count of 60 cigarettes, or an alternate count of _____ cigarettes.

    I agree to smoke my allotment of _____ cigarettes today.

_____   _____

Today's date   My signature

"Get Real/Stay Real" thought for today:
Bette Davis and Paul Henreid are both dead. Could smoking have had anything to do with it? Be that as it may, each year over 500,000 deaths—20 percent of the total in the United States—are caused by smoking.

Today I feel:

_____

_____

DAY 2 or DAY ___

My allotment for today is a count of 59 cigarettes, or an alternate count of _____ cigarettes.

    I agree to smoke my allotment of _____ cigarettes today.

_____   _____

Today's date   My signature

"Get Real/Stay Real" thought for today:
Virtually every system and function of the human body is known to be adversely affected by cigarette smoking; even organs that have no direct contact with cigarette smoke are damaged by smoking.

Today I feel:

_____

_____

Plan A
Three-Packs-Per-Day Addiction: Gradual-Cessation Smoking Log

DAY 3 or DAY ___

My allotment for today is a count of 58 cigarettes, or an alternate count of _____ cigarettes.

I agree to smoke my allotment of _____ cigarettes today.

_____   _____
Today's date   My signature

"Get Real/Stay Real" thought for today:
Cigarette smoking greatly increases the risk of pancreatic cancer, bladder cancer, colon cancer, and cancer of the cervix.

Today I feel:

_____
_____
_____

DAY 4 or DAY ___

My allotment for today is a count of 57 cigarettes, or an alternate count of _____ cigarettes.

I agree to smoke my allotment of _____ cigarettes today.

_____   _____
Today's date   My signature

"Get Real/Stay Real" thought for today:
Smoking cigarettes contributes to male impotence, female infertility, loss of eyesight, loss of hearing, and bone loss.

Today I feel:

_____
_____
_____

Plan A
Three-Packs-Per-Day Addiction:
Gradual-Cessation Smoking Log

DAY 5 or DAY ___

My allotment for today is a count of 56 cigarettes, or an alternate count of _____ cigarettes.

I agree to smoke my allotment of _____ cigarettes today.

_____   _____
Today's date   My signature

"Get Real/Stay Real" thought for today:
Only seconds after inhaling cigarette smoke, 4,000 toxic by-products are absorbed into the bloodstream and transported to every cell in the body of the smoker.

Today I feel:

_____
_____
_____

DAY 6 or DAY ___

My allotment for today is a count of 55 cigarettes, or an alternate count of _____ cigarettes.

I agree to smoke my allotment of _____ cigarettes today.

_____   _____
Today's date   My signature

"Get Real/Stay Real" thought for today:
Cigarette smoking is the leading cause of lung diseases, lung cancer, and all pulmonary illness and deaths in the United States.

Today I feel:

_____
_____
_____

Plan A
Three-Packs-Per-Day Addiction: Gradual-Cessation Smoking Log

DAY 7 or DAY ___

My allotment for today is a count of 54 cigarettes, or an alternate count of _____ cigarettes.

I agree to smoke my allotment of _____ cigarettes today.

_____   _____
Today's date   My signature

"Get Real/Stay Real" thought for today:

Almost all cases of emphysema and chronic bronchitis are caused by smoking.

Today I feel:

_____

_____

_____

DAY 8 or DAY ___

My allotment for today is a count of 53 cigarettes, or an alternate count of _____ cigarettes.

I agree to smoke my allotment of _____ cigarettes today.

_____   _____
Today's date   My signature

"Get Real/Stay Real" thought for today:

The death rate for asthmatics who smoke is almost double that of non-smoking asthmatics. Pneumonia is much more likely to be fatal in smokers of any age than in nonsmokers who contract the disease.

Today I feel:

_____

_____

_____

Plan A
Three-Packs-Per-Day Addiction:
Gradual-Cessation Smoking Log

DAY 9 or DAY ___

My allotment for today is a count of 52 cigarettes, or an alternate count of _____ cigarettes.

I agree to smoke my allotment of _____ cigarettes today.

_____   _____
Today's date   My signature

"Get Real/Stay Real" thought for today:
Smokers are more vulnerable to contracting influenza than are non-smokers; the death rate among smokers suffering from influenza is much higher than in nonsmoking persons with influenza.

Today I feel:

_____

_____

_____

DAY 10 or DAY ___

My allotment for today is a count of 51 cigarettes, or an alternate count of _____ cigarettes.

I agree to smoke my allotment of _____ cigarettes today.

_____   _____
Today's date   My signature

"Get Real/Stay Real" thought for today:
Contracting tuberculosis is far more commonplace with smokers than nonsmokers, according to scientific studies.

Today I feel:

_____

_____

_____

Plan A
Three-Packs-Per-Day Addiction:
Gradual-Cessation Smoking Log

DAY 11 or DAY ___

My allotment for today is a count of 50 cigarettes, or an alternate count of _____ cigarettes.

I agree to smoke my allotment of _____ cigarettes today.

_____   _____

Today's date   My signature

"Get Real/Stay Real" thought for today:
Cancer/smoking connections are especially strong in the regions of the lungs, head, and neck (including the esophagus, larynx, tongue, salivary glands, lips, mouth, and pharynx).

Today I feel:

_____

_____

_____

DAY 12 or DAY ___

My allotment for today is a count of 49 cigarettes, or an alternate count of _____ cigarettes.

I agree to smoke my allotment of _____ cigarettes today.

_____   _____

Today's date   My signature

"Get Real/Stay Real" thought for today:
Increasing evidence suggests that smoking plays a role in the formation of colorectal cancer and leukemia.

Today I feel:

_____

_____

_____

Plan A
Three-Packs-Per-Day Addiction:
Gradual-Cessation Smoking Log

DAY 13 or DAY ___

My allotment for today is a count of 48 cigarettes, or an alternate count of _____ cigarettes.

I agree to smoke my allotment of _____ cigarettes today.

_____   _____

Today's date   My signature

"Get Real/Stay Real" thought for today:

Genital cancer, including vulvar, cervical, and penile cancer, occurs far more frequently in smokers than in nonsmokers.

Today I feel:

_____

_____

_____

DAY 14 or DAY ___

My allotment for today is a count of 47 cigarettes, or an alternate count of _____ cigarettes.

I agree to smoke my allotment of _____ cigarettes today.

_____   _____

Today's date   My signature

"Get Real/Stay Real" thought for today:

The risk of anal cancer is eight times higher in male smokers and nine times higher in female smokers than in nonsmokers.

Today I feel:

_____

_____

_____

Plan A
Three-Packs-Per-Day Addiction:
Gradual-Cessation Smoking Log

DAY 15 or DAY ___

My allotment for today is a count of 46 cigarettes, or an alternate count of _____ cigarettes.

I agree to smoke my allotment of _____ cigarettes today.

_____   _____

Today's date   My signature

"Get Real/Stay Real" thought for today:
Smoking increases the heart rate by as much as 30 percent during the first 10 minutes of smoking.

Today I feel:

_____

_____

_____

DAY 16 or DAY ___

My allotment for today is a count of 45 cigarettes, or an alternate count of _____ cigarettes.

I agree to smoke my allotment of _____ cigarettes today.

_____   _____

Today's date   My signature

"Get Real/Stay Real" thought for today:
Smokers experience an acute increase in their blood pressure; the blood vessels constrict, forcing the heart to work harder to deliver oxygen to the heart, as well as to the rest of the body.

Today I feel:

_____

_____

_____

Plan A
Three-Packs-Per-Day Addiction:
Gradual-Cessation Smoking Log

DAY 17 or DAY ___

My allotment for today is a count of 44 cigarettes, or an alternate count of _____ cigarettes.

I agree to smoke my allotment of _____ cigarettes today.

_____   _____

Today's date   My signature

"Get Real/Stay Real" thought for today:

Smoking puts one at as much risk for developing arteriosclerosis as does high blood pressure and high blood cholesterol.

Today I feel:

_____

_____

_____

DAY 18 or DAY ___

My allotment for today is a count of 43 cigarettes, or an alternate count of _____ cigarettes.

I agree to smoke my allotment of _____ cigarettes today.

_____   _____

Today's date   My signature

"Get Real/Stay Real" thought for today:

Although doctors often prescribe aspirin to help prevent clot formation that can cause heart disease, aspirin is less effective for smokers.

Today I feel:

_____

_____

_____

Plan A
Three-Packs-Per-Day Addiction:
Gradual-Cessation Smoking Log

DAY 19 or DAY ___
My allotment for today is a count of 42 cigarettes, or an alternate count of _____ cigarettes.
I agree to smoke my allotment of _____ cigarettes today.

_____   _____
Today's date   My signature

"Get Real/Stay Real" thought for today:
Smoking causes higher levels of free fatty acids in the bloodstream, raising levels of LDL, or bad cholesterol, and lowering levels of HDL, or good cholesterol.

Today I feel:

_____
_____
_____

DAY 20 or DAY ___
My allotment for today is a count of 41 cigarettes, or an alternate count of _____ cigarettes.
I agree to smoke my allotment of _____ cigarettes today.

_____   _____
Today's date   My signature

"Get Real/Stay Real" thought for today:
Women smokers experience earlier menopause, raising heart-disease risk. Even women smokers who have not yet reached menopause have lower-than-normal estrogen levels, increasing their heart-disease risk.

Today I feel:

_____
_____
_____

Plan A
Three-Packs-Per-Day Addiction:
Gradual-Cessation Smoking Log

DAY 21 or DAY ___

My allotment for today is a count of 40 cigarettes, or an alternate count of _____ cigarettes.

I agree to smoke my allotment of _____ cigarettes today.

_____

Today's date   My signature

"Get Real/Stay Real" thought for today:

Advanced medicine is less effective for smokers who continue to smoke. After angioplasty, for example, smokers with clogged arteries are more likely to experience recurrence of the disease, and to require repeat angioplasty.

Today I feel:

_____
_____
_____

DAY 22 or DAY ___

My allotment for today is a count of 39 cigarettes, or an alternate count of _____ cigarettes.

I agree to smoke my allotment of _____ cigarettes today.

_____

Today's date   My signature

"Get Real/Stay Real" thought for today:

More smokers experience chest pain (angina) and heart attacks than do nonsmokers; strong evidence suggests that smokers experience first heart attacks earlier than nonsmokers.

Today I feel:

_____
_____
_____

Plan A
Three-Packs-Per-Day Addiction:
Gradual-Cessation Smoking Log

DAY 23 or DAY ___

My allotment for today is a count of 38 cigarettes, or an alternate count of _____ cigarettes.

I agree to smoke my allotment of _____ cigarettes today.

_____   _____

Today's date   My signature

"Get Real/Stay Real" thought for today:

Lower-tar cigarettes, contrary to popular belief, do not provide any reduction in risk for a first heart attack.

Today I feel:

_____

_____

_____

DAY 24 or DAY ___

My allotment for today is a count of 37 cigarettes, or an alternate count of _____ cigarettes.

I agree to smoke my allotment of _____ cigarettes today.

_____   _____

Today's date   My signature

"Get Real/Stay Real" thought for today:

Smoking causes an increased release of adrenaline, which can interfere with the heart's normal rhythm and cause arrhythmia or abnormal heart rhythms, increasing the chances of dying of a heart attack.

Today I feel:

_____

_____

_____

Plan A
Three-Packs-Per-Day Addiction:
Gradual-Cessation Smoking Log

DAY 25 or DAY ___

My allotment for today is a count of 36 cigarettes, or an alternate count of _____ cigarettes.

I agree to smoke my allotment of _____ cigarettes today.

_____   _____

Today's date   My signature

"Get Real/Stay Real" thought for today:

Developing cardiomyopathy is a much greater risk for smokers; carbon monoxide in cigarette smoke can damage the heart muscle directly.

Today I feel:

_____

_____

_____

DAY 26 or DAY ___

My allotment for today is a count of 35 cigarettes, or an alternate count of _____ cigarettes.

I agree to smoke my allotment of _____ cigarettes today.

_____   _____

Today's date   My signature

"Get Real/Stay Real" thought for today:

Smoking not only damages the blood vessels of the heart, it causes serious injury to blood vessels throughout the body.

Today I feel:

_____

_____

_____

Plan A
Three-Packs-Per-Day Addiction:
Gradual-Cessation Smoking Log

DAY 27 or DAY ___

My allotment for today is a count of 34 cigarettes, or an alternate count of _____ cigarettes.

I agree to smoke my allotment of _____ cigarettes today.

_____   _____

Today's date   My signature

"Get Real/Stay Real" thought for today:

Smoking injures blood vessels in the brain, leading to strokes that can cause irreversible brain damage.

Today I feel:

_____

_____

_____

DAY 28 or DAY ___

My allotment for today is a count of 33 cigarettes, or an alternate count of _____ cigarettes.

I agree to smoke my allotment of _____ cigarettes today.

_____   _____

Today's date   My signature

"Get Real/Stay Real" thought for today:

Peripheral vascular disease is overwhelmingly more prevalent in smokers (76%). In the later stages of this disease, open sores develop on the legs and feet, commonly progressing to gangrene, the death of diseased tissue; amputations are sometimes necessary.

Today I feel:

_____

_____

_____

Plan A
Three-Packs-Per-Day Addiction:
Gradual-Cessation Smoking Log

DAY 29 or DAY ___

My allotment for today is a count of 32 cigarettes, or an alternate count of _____ cigarettes.

I agree to smoke my allotment of _____ cigarettes today.

_____   _____
Today's date   My signature

"Get Real/Stay Real" thought for today:
Smokers look much older than nonsmokers; smokers in their forties have facial wrinkles similar to nonsmoking sixty-year-olds.

Today I feel:

_____
_____
_____

DAY 30 or DAY ___

My allotment for today is a count of 31 cigarettes, or an alternate count of _____ cigarettes.

I agree to smoke my allotment of _____ cigarettes today.

_____   _____
Today's date   My signature

"Get Real/Stay Real" thought for today:
Smoking constricts blood vessels, reducing the amount of blood, and the nutrients contained in blood, flowing to the skin. Smokers' facial skin has an atrophied or wasted appearance.

Today I feel:

_____
_____
_____

Plan A
Three-Packs-Per-Day Addiction:
Gradual-Cessation Smoking Log

DAY 31 or DAY ___

My allotment for today is a count of 30 cigarettes, or an alternate count of _____ cigarettes.

I agree to smoke my allotment of _____ cigarettes today.

_____   _____

Today's date   My signature

"Get Real/Stay Real" thought for today:

In addition to leathery skin, smokers characteristically have "crow's feet" around the eyes and tiny wrinkles above and below the lips. For women who wear lipstick, lipstick tends to bleed into these wrinkles.

Today I feel:

_____

_____

_____

DAY 32 or DAY ___

My allotment for today is a count of 29 cigarettes, or an alternate count of _____ cigarettes.

I agree to smoke my allotment of _____ cigarettes today.

_____   _____

Today's date   My signature

"Get Real/Stay Real" thought for today:

Smokers have a considerably higher risk for developing psoriasis, a chronic skin condition causing reddish/silvery sores that can erupt anywhere on the skin's surface.

Today I feel:

_____

_____

_____

Plan A
Three-Packs-Per-Day Addiction:
Gradual-Cessation Smoking Log

DAY 33 or DAY ___

My allotment for today is a count of 28 cigarettes, or an alternate count of _____ cigarettes.

I agree to smoke my allotment of _____ cigarettes today.

_____   _____
Today's date   My signature

"Get Real/Stay Real" thought for today:
Scientific studies have found significant associations between smoking and a type of skin cancer called squamous cell carcinoma, characterized by scaly, red outlined patches.

Today I feel:

_____
_____
_____

DAY 34 or DAY ___

My allotment for today is a count of 27 cigarettes, or an alternate count of _____ cigarettes.

I agree to smoke my allotment of _____ cigarettes today.

_____   _____
Today's date   My signature

"Get Real/Stay Real" thought for today:
Smokers have a greater risk of anesthesia complications when undergoing surgery than do nonsmokers. Smokers also require *more* anesthesia for surgery, a lengthened stay in the recovery room, and an increased need for supplemental oxygen therapy.

Today I feel:

_____
_____
_____

Plan A
Three-Packs-Per-Day Addiction:
Gradual-Cessation Smoking Log

DAY 35 or DAY ___
My allotment for today is a count of 26 cigarettes, or an alternate count of _____ cigarettes.
I agree to smoke my allotment of _____ cigarettes today.

_____   _____
Today's date   My signature

"Get Real/Stay Real" thought for today:
Scientists have known since 1977 that smoking delays wound healing; smokers have slower healing wounds overall, whether the wounds are from disease, injury, or surgery.

Today I feel:

_____
_____
_____

DAY 36 or DAY ___
My allotment for today is a count of 25 cigarettes, or an alternate count of _____ cigarettes.
I agree to smoke my allotment of _____ cigarettes today.

_____   _____
Today's date   My signature

"Get Real/Stay Real" thought for today:
Most plastic surgeons will *not* operate on smokers because in plastic and reconstructive surgery, skin flaps depend on adequate blood supply and ample oxygen flow to heal.

Today I feel:

_____
_____
_____

Plan A
Three-Packs-Per-Day Addiction:
Gradual-Cessation Smoking Log

DAY 37 or DAY ___

My allotment for today is a count of 24 cigarettes, or an alternate count of _____ cigarettes.

I agree to smoke my allotment of _____ cigarettes today.

_____   _____
Today's date   My signature

"Get Real/Stay Real" thought for today:

Smokers are subject to more bone fractures because they have higher incidents of osteoporosis (decreased bone density); fractures take considerably longer to heal.

Today I feel:

_____
_____
_____

DAY 38 or DAY ___

My allotment for today is a count of 23 cigarettes, or an alternate count of _____ cigarettes.

I agree to smoke my allotment of _____ cigarettes today.

_____   _____
Today's date   My signature

"Get Real/Stay Real" thought for today:

The association between smoking, back pain, and musculoskeletal injuries is so well established that prevention of back pain has been shown to be a beneficial side effect of not smoking.

Today I feel:

_____
_____
_____

Plan A
Three-Packs-Per-Day Addiction:
Gradual-Cessation Smoking Log

DAY 39 or DAY ___

My allotment for today is a count of 22 cigarettes, or an alternate count of _____ cigarettes.

I agree to smoke my allotment of _____ cigarettes today.

_____   _____
Today's date   My signature

"Get Real/Stay Real" thought for today:
Risk for brittle bones doesn't take a lifetime to develop in smokers. Scientists report that one disturbing study shows a lower bone mineral density in case studies of teenage girls who smoked as opposed to those girls in the study who were nonsmokers.

Today I feel:

_____

_____

_____

DAY 40 or DAY ___

My allotment for today is a count of 21 cigarettes, or an alternate count of _____ cigarettes.

I agree to smoke my allotment of _____ cigarettes today.

_____   _____
Today's date   My signature

"Get Real/Stay Real" thought for today:
Household "passive smoking," as it is called, results in hundreds of thousands of cases of bronchitis, pneumonia, ear infections, and worsened asthma in children.

Today I feel:

_____

_____

_____

Plan A
Three-Packs-Per-Day Addiction: Gradual-Cessation Smoking Log

DAY 41 or DAY ___

My allotment for today is a count of 20 cigarettes, or an alternate count of _____ cigarettes.

I agree to smoke my allotment of _____ cigarettes today.

_____   _____

Today's date   My signature

"Get Real/Stay Real" thought for today:

Becoming pregnant and maintaining pregnancy is far more difficult for smokers than nonsmokers. Doctors use the term "fetal tobacco syndrome" in order to provide uniform diagnostic criteria.

Today I feel:

_____
_____
_____

DAY 42 or DAY ___

My allotment for today is a count of 19 cigarettes, or an alternate count of _____ cigarettes.

I agree to smoke my allotment of _____ cigarettes today.

_____   _____

Today's date   My signature

"Get Real/Stay Real" thought for today:

Fertility rates of women who smoke are about 30 percent lower than those of nonsmoking women; female smokers are shown to be estrogen-deficient and also experience more hormonal irregularities.

Today I feel:

_____
_____
_____

Plan A
Three-Packs-Per-Day Addiction:
Gradual-Cessation Smoking Log

DAY 43 or DAY ___

My allotment for today is a count of 18 cigarettes, or an alternate count of _____ cigarettes.

I agree to smoke my allotment of _____ cigarettes today.

_____   _____

Today's date   My signature

"Get Real/Stay Real" thought for today:

Pregnant smokers are more likely to miscarry than pregnant non-smokers. Carbon monoxide and nicotine in cigarette smoke cause adverse fetal effects.

Today I feel:

_____

_____

_____

DAY 44 or DAY ___

My allotment for today is a count of 17 cigarettes, or an alternate count of _____ cigarettes.

I agree to smoke my allotment of _____ cigarettes today.

_____   _____

Today's date   My signature

"Get Real/Stay Real" thought for today:

Women smokers are more prone to their "water breaking" too early in pregnancy, bringing about premature labor. Even if a woman does not go into labor, premature rupture of her fluid-containing sac allows potentially hazardous bacteria to enter the heretofore protected environment of the fetus.

Today I feel:

_____

_____

_____

Plan A
Three-Packs-Per-Day Addiction:
Gradual-Cessation Smoking Log

DAY 45 or DAY ___
My allotment for today is a count of 16 cigarettes, or an alternate
count of _____ cigarettes.
I agree to smoke my allotment of _____ cigarettes today.

_____   _____
Today's date   My signature

"Get Real/Stay Real" thought for today:
Premature births are 20 percent more common in women who smoke
one pack of cigarettes daily than in nonsmokers. About 26,000 infants
of mothers who smoke are admitted to neonatal intensive-care units
every year. Smokers have an increased risk of delivering stillborn babies.

Today I feel:

_____
_____
_____

DAY 46 or DAY ___
My allotment for today is a count of 15 cigarettes, or an alternate
count of _____ cigarettes.
I agree to smoke my allotment of _____ cigarettes today.

_____   _____
Today's date   My signature

"Get Real/Stay Real" thought for today:
Mothers who smoke give birth to smaller, less healthy babies than do
nonsmokers. Smoking during pregnancy is the single most important
cause of poor fetal health in all developed countries.

Today I feel:

_____
_____
_____

Plan A
Three-Packs-Per-Day Addiction:
Gradual-Cessation Smoking Log

DAY 47 or DAY ___

My allotment for today is a count of 14 cigarettes, or an alternate count of _____ cigarettes.

I agree to smoke my allotment of _____ cigarettes today.

_____   _____
Today's date   My signature

"Get Real/Stay Real" thought for today:

Children of smokers experience more cognitive and behavioral problems than do children of nonsmokers. Consequently, children of smokers have a decreased ability to achieve in school.

Today I feel:

_____

_____

_____

DAY 48 or DAY ___

My allotment for today is a count of 13 cigarettes, or an alternate count of _____ cigarettes.

I agree to smoke my allotment of _____ cigarettes today.

_____   _____
Today's date   My signature

"Get Real/Stay Real" thought for today:

Scientific evidence shows that smoking decreases sperm production in men, deforms sperm, impedes the ability of sperm to move, and seriously reduces blood flow to the penis, sometimes causing impotence.

Today I feel:

_____

_____

_____

Plan A
Three-Packs-Per-Day Addiction:
Gradual-Cessation Smoking Log

DAY 49 or DAY ___

My allotment for today is a count of 12 cigarettes, or an alternate count of _____ cigarettes.

I agree to smoke my allotment of _____ cigarettes today.

_____   _____

Today's date   My signature

"Get Real/Stay Real" thought for today:

In a 1934 laboratory experiment, researchers were able to paralyze nerves by applying nicotine directly to them. Today's research regarding the neurological problems produced via smoking is just as alarming.

Today I feel:

_____

_____

_____

DAY 50 or DAY ___

My allotment for today is a count of 11 cigarettes, or an alternate count of _____ cigarettes.

I agree to smoke my allotment of _____ cigarettes today.

_____   _____

Today's date   My signature

"Get Real/Stay Real" thought for today:

At least 61,500 strokes could be *prevented* each year if people stopped smoking. The economic impact alone would be staggering; an enormous savings of $3 billion would result.

Today I feel:

_____

_____

_____

Plan A
Three-Packs-Per-Day Addiction:
Gradual-Cessation Smoking Log

DAY 51 or DAY ___

My allotment for today is a count of 10 cigarettes, or an alternate count of _____ cigarettes.

I agree to smoke my allotment of _____ cigarettes today.

_____   _____
Today's date   My signature

"Get Real/Stay Real" thought for today:
Smokers have an increased risk of hearing loss: Sudden hearing loss is experienced an average of sixteen years earlier in smokers than in non-smokers and there is a direct correlation between smoking and hearing loss caused by chronic exposure to loud noise.

Today I feel:

_____

_____

_____

DAY 52 or DAY ___

My allotment for today is a count of 9 cigarettes, or an alternate count of _____ cigarettes.

I agree to smoke my allotment of _____ cigarettes today.

_____   _____
Today's date   My signature

"Get Real/Stay Real" thought for today:
Experts agree that smoking worsens chronic inflammation of the nose, worsening symptoms of sneezing, nasal congestion, and a running, itching nose.

Today I feel:

_____

_____

_____

Plan A
Three-Packs-Per-Day Addiction: Gradual-Cessation Smoking Log

DAY 53 or DAY ___

My allotment for today is a count of 8 cigarettes, or an alternate count of _____ cigarettes.

I agree to smoke my allotment of _____ cigarettes today.

_____   _____
Today's date   My signature

"Get Real/Stay Real" thought for today:

Smokers are at least twice as likely to develop cataracts than non-smokers of similar age. Smokers with Grave's disease, characterized by symptoms including double vision and eye-muscle abnormalities, are eight times more likely to develop the severe complications associated with this disease than are nonsmokers.

Today I feel:

_____
_____
_____

DAY 54 or DAY ___

My allotment for today is a count of 7 cigarettes, or an alternate count of _____ cigarettes.

I agree to smoke my allotment of _____ cigarettes today.

_____   _____
Today's date   My signature

"Get Real/Stay Real" thought for today:

Smoking affects the mouth's environment adversely by changing saliva and slowing its production, impeding the flush-away process of bacteria and wastes.

Today I feel:

_____
_____
_____

Plan A
Three-Packs-Per-Day Addiction:
Gradual-Cessation Smoking Log

DAY 55 or DAY ___

My allotment for today is a count of 6 cigarettes, or an alternate count of _____ cigarettes.

I agree to smoke my allotment of _____ cigarettes today.

_____   _____

Today's date   My signature

"Get Real/Stay Real" thought for today:

Smoking stimulates accumulation of calcified deposits that form on the teeth, plaque, and staining of the teeth.

Today I feel:

_____

_____

_____

DAY 56 or DAY ___

My allotment for today is a count of 5 cigarettes, or an alternate count of _____ cigarettes.

I agree to smoke my allotment of _____ cigarettes today.

_____   _____

Today's date   My signature

"Get Real/Stay Real" thought for today:

Smoking raises the temperature in the mouth from a normal 98.6° F to 107.6° F. At this temperature, cells are damaged and eventually die.

Today I feel:

_____

_____

_____

Plan A
Three-Packs-Per-Day Addiction:
Gradual-Cessation Smoking Log

DAY 57 or DAY ___

My allotment for today is a count of 4 cigarettes, or an alternate count of _____ cigarettes.

I agree to smoke my allotment of _____ cigarettes today.

_____   _____

Today's date   My signature

"Get Real/Stay Real" thought for today:

Smoking breaks down vitamin C, adversely affecting soft tissues within the mouth, impairing their ability to heal, leading to gum diseases. Smokers are far more likely than nonsmokers to develop periodontal diseases and experience bone loss and loss of teeth.

Today I feel:

_____

_____

_____

DAY 58 or DAY ___

My allotment for today is a count of 3 cigarettes, or an alternate count of _____ cigarettes.

I agree to smoke my allotment of _____ cigarettes today.

_____   _____

Today's date   My signature

"Get Real/Stay Real" thought for today:

Smoking increases the risk of stomach ulcers. Smokers have significantly more gastric reflux than do nonsmokers. When acid from a smoker's stomach backs up, it causes heartburn and increases the chance of developing an ulcer.

Today I feel:

_____

_____

_____

Plan A
Three-Packs-Per-Day Addiction:
Gradual-Cessation Smoking Log

DAY 59 or DAY ____

My allotment for today is a count of 2 cigarettes, or an alternate count of _____ cigarettes.

I agree to smoke my allotment of _____ cigarettes today.

---------------------   ---

Today's date   My signature

"Get Real/Stay Real" thought for today:

Smoking increases the risk of developing colon polyps (growths in the colon). This risk is important because some colon polyps go on to become cancerous.

Today I feel:

_____

_____

_____

DAY 60 or DAY ____   FINAL DAY

My allotment for today is a count of 1 cigarette. An alternate count of _____ cigarettes.

I agree to smoke my allotment of _____ cigarettes today.

---------------------   ---

Today's date   My signature

"Get Real/Stay Real" thought for today:

Smoking impairs the immune system, increasing smokers' risk of experiencing allergic reactions and respiratory infections. Smokers have fewer natural killer cells to check viruses, so they are more at risk of acquiring epidemic influenza, and some studies suggest that smoking causes HIV-1-infected persons to progress more quickly to AIDS.

Plan A
Three-Packs-Per-Day Addiction:
Gradual-Cessation Smoking Log

Congratulations! You have successfully completed
your smoking-cessation program!
Now, turn to page 141 to begin the first 90 days of
your new *smoke-free* life!

Plan B
Two-Packs-Per-Day Addiction:
Gradual-Cessation Smoking Log

DAY 1 or DAY ___

I typically smoke two packs of cigarettes in a 24-hour period. My allotment for today is a count of 40 cigarettes, or an alternate count of _____ cigarettes.

I agree to smoke my allotment of _____ cigarettes today.

_____   _____

Today's date   My signature

"Get Real/Stay Real" thought for today:

Bette Davis and Paul Henreid are both dead. Could smoking have had anything to do with it? Be that as it may, each year over 500,000 deaths—20 percent of the total in the United States—are caused by smoking.

Today I feel:

_____

_____

_____

DAY 2 or DAY ___

My allotment for today is a count of 39 cigarettes, or an alternate count of _____ cigarettes.

I agree to smoke my allotment of _____ cigarettes today.

_____   _____

Today's date   My signature

"Get Real/Stay Real" thought for today:

Virtually every system and function of the human body is known to be adversely affected by cigarette smoking; even organs that have no direct contact with cigarette smoke are damaged by smoking.

Today I feel:

_____

_____

Plan B
Two-Packs-Per-Day Addiction:
Gradual-Cessation Smoking Log

DAY 3 or DAY ___
My allotment for today is a count of 38 cigarettes, or an alternate count of _____ cigarettes.
I agree to smoke my allotment of _____ cigarettes today.

Today's date   My signature

"Get Real/Stay Real" thought for today:
Cigarette smoking greatly increases the risk of pancreatic cancer, bladder cancer, colon cancer, and cancer of the cervix.

Today I feel:

DAY 4 or DAY ___
My allotment for today is a count of 37 cigarettes, or an alternate count of _____ cigarettes.
I agree to smoke my allotment of _____ cigarettes today.

Today's date   My signature

"Get Real/Stay Real" thought for today:
Smoking cigarettes contributes to male impotence, female infertility, loss of eyesight, loss of hearing, and bone loss.

Today I feel:

Plan B
Two-Packs-Per-Day Addiction:
Gradual-Cessation Smoking Log

DAY 5 or DAY ___
My allotment for today is a count of 36 cigarettes, or an alternate count of _____ cigarettes.
I agree to smoke my allotment of _____ cigarettes today.

_____ _____
Today's date   My signature

"Get Real/Stay Real" thought for today:
Only seconds after inhaling cigarette smoke, 4,000 toxic by-products are absorbed into the bloodstream and transported to every cell in the body of the smoker.

Today I feel:

_____
_____
_____

DAY 6 or DAY ___
My allotment for today is a count of 35 cigarettes, or an alternate count of _____ cigarettes.
I agree to smoke my allotment of _____ cigarettes today.

_____ _____
Today's date   My signature

"Get Real/Stay Real" thought for today:
Cigarette smoking is the leading cause of lung diseases, lung cancer, and all pulmonary illness and deaths in the United States.

Today I feel:

_____
_____

Plan B
Two-Packs-Per-Day Addiction:
Gradual-Cessation Smoking Log

DAY 7 or DAY ___
My allotment for today is a count of 34 cigarettes, or an alternate count of _____ cigarettes.
I agree to smoke my allotment of _____ cigarettes today.

_____   _____
Today's date   My signature

"Get Real/Stay Real" thought for today:
Almost all cases of emphysema and chronic bronchitis are caused by smoking.

Today I feel:

_____
_____
_____

DAY 8 or DAY ___
My allotment for today is a count of 33 cigarettes, or an alternate count of _____ cigarettes.
I agree to smoke my allotment of _____ cigarettes today.

_____   _____
Today's date   My signature

"Get Real/Stay Real" thought for today:
The death rate for asthmatics who smoke is almost double that of non-smoking asthmatics. Pneumonia is much more likely to be fatal in smokers of any age than in nonsmokers who contract the disease.

Today I feel:

_____
_____

Plan B
Two-Packs-Per-Day Addiction:
Gradual-Cessation Smoking Log

DAY 9 or DAY ___

My allotment for today is a count of 32 cigarettes, or an alternate count of _____ cigarettes.

I agree to smoke my allotment of _____ cigarettes today.

_____   _____
Today's date   My signature

"Get Real/Stay Real" thought for today:

Smokers are more vulnerable to contracting influenza than are non-smokers; the death rate among smokers suffering from influenza is much higher than in nonsmoking persons with influenza.

Today I feel:

_____
_____
_____

DAY 10 or DAY ___

My allotment for today is a count of 31 cigarettes, or an alternate count of _____ cigarettes.

I agree to smoke my allotment of _____ cigarettes today.

_____   _____
Today's date   My signature

"Get Real/Stay Real" thought for today:

Tuberculosis is far more common with smokers than nonsmokers, according to scientific studies.

Today I feel:

_____
_____

Plan B
Two-Packs-Per-Day Addiction:
Gradual-Cessation Smoking Log

DAY 11 or DAY ___

My allotment for today is a count of 30 cigarettes, or an alternate count of _____ cigarettes.

I agree to smoke my allotment of _____ cigarettes today.

_____   _____

Today's date   My signature

"Get Real/Stay Real" thought for today:

Cancer/smoking connections are especially strong in the regions of the lungs, head, and neck (including the esophagus, larynx, tongue, salivary glands, lips, mouth, and pharynx).

Today I feel:

_____

_____

_____

DAY 12 or DAY ___

My allotment for today is a count of 29 cigarettes, or an alternate count of _____ cigarettes.

I agree to smoke my allotment of _____ cigarettes today.

_____   _____

Today's date   My signature

"Get Real/Stay Real" thought for today:

Increasing evidence suggests that smoking plays a role in the formation of colorectal cancer and leukemia.

Today I feel:

_____

_____

Plan B
Two-Packs-Per-Day Addiction:
Gradual-Cessation Smoking Log

DAY 13 or DAY ___
My allotment for today is a count of 28 cigarettes, or an alternate count of _____ cigarettes.
I agree to smoke my allotment of _____ cigarettes today.

_____   _____
Today's date   My signature

"Get Real/Stay Real" thought for today:
Genital cancer, including vulvar, cervical, and penile cancer, occurs far more frequently in smokers than in nonsmokers.

Today I feel:

_____
_____
_____

DAY 14 or DAY ___
My allotment for today is a count of 27 cigarettes, or an alternate count of _____ cigarettes.
I agree to smoke my allotment of _____ cigarettes today.

_____   _____
Today's date   My signature

"Get Real/Stay Real" thought for today:
The risk of anal cancer is eight times higher in male smokers and nine times higher in female smokers than in nonsmokers.

Today I feel:

_____
_____

Plan B
Two-Packs-Per-Day Addiction:
Gradual-Cessation Smoking Log

DAY 15 or DAY ___

My allotment for today is a count of 26 cigarettes, or an alternate count of _____ cigarettes.

I agree to smoke my allotment of _____ cigarettes today.

_____   _____
Today's date   My signature

"Get Real/Stay Real" thought for today:
Smoking increases the heart rate by as much as 30 percent during the first 10 minutes of smoking.

Today I feel:

_____

_____

DAY 16 or DAY ___

My allotment for today is a count of 25 cigarettes, or an alternate count of _____ cigarettes.

I agree to smoke my allotment of _____ cigarettes today.

_____   _____
Today's date   My signature

"Get Real/Stay Real" thought for today:
Smokers experience an acute increase in their blood pressure; the blood vessels constrict, forcing the heart to work harder to deliver oxygen to the heart, as well as to the rest of the body.

Today I feel:

_____

_____

Plan B
Two-Packs-Per-Day Addiction:
Gradual-Cessation Smoking Log

DAY 17 or DAY ___
My allotment for today is a count of 24 cigarettes, or an alternate count of _____ cigarettes.
I agree to smoke my allotment of _____ cigarettes today.

Today's date   My signature

"Get Real/Stay Real" thought for today:
Smoking puts one at as much risk for developing arteriosclerosis as does high blood pressure and high blood cholesterol.

Today I feel:

DAY 18 or DAY ___
My allotment for today is a count of 23 cigarettes, or an alternate count of _____ cigarettes.
I agree to smoke my allotment of _____ cigarettes today.

Today's date   My signature

"Get Real/Stay Real" thought for today:
Although doctors often prescribe aspirin to help prevent clot formation that can cause heart disease, aspirin is less effective for smokers.

Today I feel:

Plan B
Two-Packs-Per-Day Addiction:
Gradual-Cessation Smoking Log

DAY 19 or DAY ___
My allotment for today is a count of 22 cigarettes, or an alternate count of _____ cigarettes.
I agree to smoke my allotment of _____ cigarettes today.

_____   _____
Today's date   My signature

"Get Real/Stay Real" thought for today:
Smoking causes higher levels of free fatty acids in the bloodstream, raising levels of LDL, or bad cholesterol, and lowering levels of HDL, or good cholesterol.

Today I feel:

_____
_____
_____

DAY 20 or DAY ___
My allotment for today is a count of 21 cigarettes, or an alternate count of _____ cigarettes.
I agree to smoke my allotment of _____ cigarettes today.

_____   _____
Today's date   My signature

"Get Real/Stay Real" thought for today:
Women smokers experience earlier menopause, raising heart-disease risk. Even women smokers who have not yet reached menopause have lower-than-normal estrogen levels, increasing their heart-disease risk.

Today I feel:

_____

Plan B
Two-Packs-Per-Day Addiction: Gradual-Cessation Smoking Log

_____

_____

DAY 21 or DAY ___

My allotment for today is a count of 20 cigarettes, or an alternate count of _____ cigarettes.

I agree to smoke my allotment of _____ cigarettes today.

_____   _____

Today's date   My signature

"Get Real/Stay Real" thought for today:

Advanced medicine is less effective for smokers who continue to smoke. After angioplasty, for example, smokers with clogged arteries are more likely to experience recurrence of the disease and to require repeat angioplasty.

Today I feel:

_____

_____

_____

DAY 22 or DAY ___

My allotment for today is a count of 19 cigarettes, or an alternate count of _____ cigarettes.

I agree to smoke my allotment of _____ cigarettes today.

_____   _____

Today's date   My signature

"Get Real/Stay Real" thought for today:

More smokers experience chest pain (angina) and heart attacks than do nonsmokers; strong evidence suggests that smokers experience first heart attacks earlier than nonsmokers.

Plan B
Two-Packs-Per-Day Addiction:
Gradual-Cessation Smoking Log

Today I feel:

_____

_____

_____

DAY 23 or DAY ___

My allotment for today is a count of 18 cigarettes, or an alternate count of _____ cigarettes.

I agree to smoke my allotment of _____ cigarettes today.

_____   _____
Today's date   My signature

"Get Real/Stay Real" thought for today:

Lower-tar cigarettes, contrary to popular belief, do not provide any reduction in risk for a first heart attack.

Today I feel:

_____

_____

_____

DAY 24 or DAY ___

My allotment for today is a count of 17 cigarettes, or an alternate count of _____ cigarettes.

I agree to smoke my allotment of _____ cigarettes today.

_____   _____
Today's date   My signature

"Get Real/Stay Real" thought for today:

Smoking causes an increased release of adrenaline, which can interfere with the heart's normal rhythm and cause arrhythmia or abnormal heart rhythms, increasing the chances of dying of a heart attack.

Plan B
Two-Packs-Per-Day Addiction:
Gradual-Cessation Smoking Log

Today I feel:

_____

_____

_____

DAY 25 or DAY ___

My allotment for today is a count of 16 cigarettes, or an alternate count of _____ cigarettes.

I agree to smoke my allotment of _____ cigarettes today.

_____   _____

Today's date   My signature

"Get Real/Stay Real" thought for today:

Developing cardiomyopathy is a much greater risk for smokers; carbon monoxide in cigarette smoke can damage the heart muscle directly.

Today I feel:

_____

_____

_____

DAY 26 or DAY ___

My allotment for today is a count of 15 cigarettes, or an alternate count of _____ cigarettes.

I agree to smoke my allotment of _____ cigarettes today.

_____   _____

Today's date   My signature

"Get Real/Stay Real" thought for today:

Smoking not only damages the blood vessels of the heart, it causes serious injury to blood vessels throughout the body.

Plan B
Two-Packs-Per-Day Addiction:
Gradual-Cessation Smoking Log

Today I feel:

_____

_____

_____

DAY 27 or DAY ___

My allotment for today is a count of 14 cigarettes, or an alternate count of _____ cigarettes.

I agree to smoke my allotment of _____ cigarettes today.

_____   _____

Today's date   My signature

"Get Real/Stay Real" thought for today:
Smoking injures blood vessels in the brain, leading to strokes that can cause irreversible brain damage.

Today I feel:

_____

_____

_____

DAY 28 or DAY ___

My allotment for today is a count of 13 cigarettes, or an alternate count of _____ cigarettes.

I agree to smoke my allotment of _____ cigarettes today.

_____   _____

Today's date   My signature

"Get Real/Stay Real" thought for today:
Peripheral vascular disease is overwhelmingly more prevalent in smokers (76%). In the later stages of this disease, open sores develop on the legs and feet, commonly progressing to gangrene, the death of diseased tissue; amputations are sometimes necessary.

Plan B
Two-Packs-Per-Day Addiction:
Gradual-Cessation Smoking Log

Today I feel:

_____

_____

_____

DAY 29 or DAY ___

My allotment for today is a count of 12 cigarettes, or an alternate count of _____ cigarettes.

I agree to smoke my allotment of _____ cigarettes today.

_____   _____

Today's date   My signature

"Get Real/Stay Real" thought for today:
Smokers look much older than nonsmokers; smokers in their forties have facial wrinkles similar to nonsmoking sixty-year-olds.

Today I feel:

_____

_____

_____

DAY 30 or DAY ___

My allotment for today is a count of 11 cigarettes, or an alternate count of _____ cigarettes.

I agree to smoke my allotment of _____ cigarettes today.

_____   _____

Today's date   My signature

"Get Real/Stay Real" thought for today:
Smoking constricts blood vessels, reducing the amount of blood, and the nutrients contained in blood, flowing to the skin. Smokers' facial skin has an atrophied or wasted appearance.

Plan B
Two-Packs-Per-Day Addiction:
Gradual-Cessation Smoking Log

Today I feel:

_____

_____

_____

DAY 31 or DAY ___

My allotment for today is a count of 10 cigarettes, or an alternate count of _____ cigarettes.

I agree to smoke my allotment of _____ cigarettes today.

_____   _____

Today's date   My signature

"Get Real/Stay Real" thought for today:
In addition to leathery skin, smokers characteristically have "crow's feet" around the eyes and tiny wrinkles above and below the lips. For women who wear lipstick, lipstick tends to bleed into these wrinkles.

Today I feel:

_____

_____

_____

DAY 32 or DAY ___

My allotment for today is a count of 9 cigarettes, or an alternate count of _____ cigarettes.

I agree to smoke my allotment of _____ cigarettes today.

_____   _____

Today's date   My signature

"Get Real/Stay Real" thought for today:
Smokers have a considerably higher risk for developing psoriasis, a chronic skin condition causing reddish/silvery sores that can erupt anywhere on the skin's surface.

Plan B
Two-Packs-Per-Day Addiction:
Gradual-Cessation Smoking Log

Today I feel:

_____

_____

_____

DAY 33 or DAY ___

My allotment for today is a count of 8 cigarettes, or an alternate count of _____ cigarettes.

I agree to smoke my allotment of _____ cigarettes today.

_____   _____

Today's date   My signature

"Get Real/Stay Real" thought for today:

Scientific studies have found significant associations between smoking and a type of skin cancer called squamous cell carcinoma, characterized by scaly, red outlined patches.

Today I feel:

_____

_____

_____

DAY 34 or DAY ___

My allotment for today is a count of 7 cigarettes, or an alternate count of _____ cigarettes.

I agree to smoke my allotment of _____ cigarettes today.

_____   _____

Today's date   My signature

"Get Real/Stay Real" thought for today:

Smokers have a greater risk of anesthesia complications when undergoing surgery than do nonsmokers. Smokers also require *more* anesthesia for surgery, a lengthened stay in the recovery room, and an increased need for supplemental oxygen therapy.

Plan B
Two-Packs-Per-Day Addiction:
Gradual-Cessation Smoking Log

Today I feel:

_____

_____

_____

DAY 35 or DAY ___

My allotment for today is a count of 6 cigarettes, or an alternate count of _____ cigarettes.

I agree to smoke my allotment of _____ cigarettes today.

_____   _____

Today's date   My signature

"Get Real/Stay Real" thought for today:
Scientists have known since 1977 that smoking delays wound healing; smokers have slower healing wounds overall, whether the wounds are from disease, injury, or surgery.

Today I feel:

_____

_____

_____

DAY 36 or DAY ___

My allotment for today is a count of 5 cigarettes, or an alternate count of _____ cigarettes.

I agree to smoke my allotment of _____ cigarettes today.

_____   _____

Today's date   My signature

"Get Real/Stay Real" thought for today:
Most plastic surgeons will *not* operate on smokers because in plastic and reconstructive surgery, skin flaps depend on adequate blood supply and ample oxygen flow to heal.

Plan B
Two-Packs-Per-Day Addiction:
Gradual-Cessation Smoking Log

Today I feel:

_____

_____

_____

DAY 37 or DAY ___

My allotment for today is a count of 4 cigarettes, or an alternate count of _____ cigarettes.

I agree to smoke my allotment of _____ cigarettes today.

_____   _____

Today's date   My signature

"Get Real/Stay Real" thought for today:

Smokers are subject to more bone fractures because they have higher incidents of osteoporosis (decreased bone density); fractures take considerably longer to heal.

Today I feel:

_____

_____

_____

DAY 38 or DAY ___

My allotment for today is a count of 3 cigarettes, or an alternate count of _____ cigarettes.

I agree to smoke my allotment of _____ cigarettes today.

_____   _____

Today's date   My signature

"Get Real/Stay Real" thought for today:

The association between smoking, back pain, and musculoskeletal injuries is so well established that prevention of back pain has been shown to be a beneficial side effect of not smoking.

Plan B
Two-Packs-Per-Day Addiction:
Gradual-Cessation Smoking Log

Today I feel:

_____

_____

_____

DAY 39 or DAY ___

My allotment for today is a count of 2 cigarettes, or an alternate count
of _____ cigarettes.

I agree to smoke my allotment of _____ cigarettes today.

_____   _____

Today's date   My signature

"Get Real/Stay Real" thought for today:

Risk for brittle bones doesn't take a lifetime to develop in smokers.
Scientists report that one disturbing study shows a lower bone mineral
density in case studies of teenage girls who smoked as opposed to those
girls in the study who were nonsmokers.

Today I feel:

_____

_____

_____

DAY 40 or DAY ___   FINAL DAY

My allotment for today is a count of 1 cigarette. An alternate count of
_____ cigarettes.

I agree to smoke my allotment of _____ cigarettes today.

_____   _____

Today's date   My signature

Plan B
Two-Packs-Per-Day Addiction:
Gradual-Cessation Smoking Log

"Get Real/Stay Real" thought for today:
Household "passive smoking," as it is called, results in hundreds of thousands of cases of bronchitis, pneumonia, ear infections, and worsened asthma in children.

Congratulations! You have successfully completed
your smoking-cessation program!
Now, turn to page 141 to begin the first 90 days of
your new *smoke-free* life!

Plan C
One-Pack-Per-Day Addiction:
Gradual-Cessation Smoking Log

DAY 1 or DAY ____

I typically smoke one pack of cigarettes in a 24-hour period. My allotment for today is a count of 20 cigarettes, or an alternate count of _____ cigarettes.

I agree to smoke my allotment of _____ cigarettes today.

_____   _____

Today's date   My signature

"Get Real/Stay Real" thought for today:

Bette Davis and Paul Henreid are both dead. Could smoking have had anything to do with it? Be that as it may, each year over 500,000 deaths —20 percent of the total in the United States—are caused by smoking.

Today I feel:

_____

_____

_____

DAY 2 or DAY ____

My allotment for today is a count of 19 cigarettes, or an alternate count of _____ cigarettes.

I agree to smoke my allotment of _____ cigarettes today.

_____   _____

Today's date   My signature

"Get Real/Stay Real" thought for today:

Virtually every system and function of the human body is known to be adversely affected by cigarette smoking; even organs that have no direct contact with cigarette smoke are damaged by smoking.

Today I feel:

_____

_____

_____

Plan C
One-Pack-Per-Day Addiction:
Gradual-Cessation Smoking Log

DAY 3 or DAY ___
My allotment for today is a count of 18 cigarettes, or an alternate count of _____ cigarettes.
I agree to smoke my allotment of _____ cigarettes today.

_____   _____

Today's date   My signature

"Get Real/Stay Real" thought for today:
Cigarette smoking greatly increases the risk of pancreatic cancer, bladder cancer, colon cancer, and cancer of the cervix.

Today I feel:

_____

_____

_____

DAY 4 or DAY ___
My allotment for today is a count of 17 cigarettes, or an alternate count of _____ cigarettes.
I agree to smoke my allotment of _____ cigarettes today.

_____   _____

Today's date   My signature

"Get Real/Stay Real" thought for today:
Smoking cigarettes contributes to male impotence, female infertility, loss of eyesight, loss of hearing, and bone loss.

Today I feel:

_____

_____

_____

Plan C
One-Pack-Per-Day Addiction:
Gradual-Cessation Smoking Log

DAY 5 or DAY ___

My allotment for today is a count of 16 cigarettes, or an alternate count of _____ cigarettes.

I agree to smoke my allotment of _____ cigarettes today.

_____   _____

Today's date   My signature

"Get Real/Stay Real" thought for today:

Only seconds after inhaling cigarette smoke, 4,000 toxic by-products are absorbed into the bloodstream and transported to every cell in the body of the smoker.

Today I feel:

_____

_____

_____

DAY 6 or DAY ___

My allotment for today is a count of 15 cigarettes, or an alternate count of _____ cigarettes.

I agree to smoke my allotment of _____ cigarettes today.

_____   _____

Today's date   My signature

"Get Real/Stay Real" thought for today:

Cigarette smoking is the leading cause of lung diseases, lung cancer, and all pulmonary illness and deaths in the United States.

Today I feel:

_____

_____

_____

Plan C
One-Pack-Per-Day Addiction:
Gradual-Cessation Smoking Log

DAY 7 or DAY ___

My allotment for today is a count of 14 cigarettes, or an alternate count of _____ cigarettes.

I agree to smoke my allotment of _____ cigarettes today.

_____   _____

Today's date   My signature

"Get Real/Stay Real" thought for today:

Almost all cases of emphysema and chronic bronchitis are caused by smoking.

Today I feel:

_____

_____

_____

DAY 8 or DAY ___

My allotment for today is a count of 13 cigarettes, or an alternate count of _____ cigarettes.

I agree to smoke my allotment of _____ cigarettes today.

_____   _____

Today's date   My signature

"Get Real/Stay Real" thought for today:

The death rate for asthmatics who smoke is almost double that of non-smoking asthmatics. Pneumonia is much more likely to be fatal in smokers of any age than in nonsmokers who contract the disease.

Today I feel:

_____

_____

_____

Plan C
One-Pack-Per-Day Addiction:
Gradual-Cessation Smoking Log

DAY 9 or DAY ___

My allotment for today is a count of 12 cigarettes, or an alternate count of _____ cigarettes.

I agree to smoke my allotment of _____ cigarettes today.

_____   _____

Today's date   My signature

"Get Real/Stay Real" thought for today:

Smokers are more vulnerable to contracting influenza than are nonsmokers; the death rate among smokers suffering from influenza is much higher than in nonsmoking persons with influenza.

Today I feel:

_____

_____

_____

DAY 10 or DAY ___

My allotment for today is a count of 11 cigarettes, or an alternate count of _____ cigarettes.

I agree to smoke my allotment of _____ cigarettes today.

_____   _____

Today's date   My signature

"Get Real/Stay Real" thought for today:

Tuberculosis is far more common with smokers than nonsmokers, according to scientific studies.

Today I feel:

_____

_____

_____

Plan C
One-Pack-Per-Day Addiction:
Gradual-Cessation Smoking Log

DAY 11 or DAY ___

My allotment for today is a count of 10 cigarettes, or an alternate count of _____ cigarettes.

I agree to smoke my allotment of _____ cigarettes today.

_____   _____

Today's date   My signature

"Get Real/Stay Real" thought for today:

Cancer/smoking connections are especially strong in the regions of the lungs, head, and neck (including the esophagus, larynx, tongue, salivary glands, lips, mouth, and pharynx).

Today I feel:

_____

_____

_____

DAY 12 or DAY ___

My allotment for today is a count of 9 cigarettes, or an alternate count of _____ cigarettes.

I agree to smoke my allotment of _____ cigarettes today.

_____   _____

Today's date   My signature

"Get Real/Stay Real" thought for today:

Increasing evidence suggests that smoking plays a role in the formation of colorectal cancer and leukemia.

Today I feel:

_____

_____

_____

Plan C
One-Pack-Per-Day Addiction:
Gradual-Cessation Smoking Log

DAY 13 or DAY ___

My allotment for today is a count of 8 cigarettes, or an alternate count of _____ cigarettes.

I agree to smoke my allotment of _____ cigarettes today.

_____   _____
Today's date   My signature

"Get Real/Stay Real" thought for today:
Genital cancer, including vulvar, cervical, and penile cancer, occurs far more frequently in smokers than in nonsmokers.

Today I feel:

_____
_____
_____

DAY 14 or DAY ___

My allotment for today is a count of 7 cigarettes, or an alternate count of _____ cigarettes.

I agree to smoke my allotment of _____ cigarettes today.

_____   _____
Today's date   My signature

"Get Real/Stay Real" thought for today:
The risk of anal cancer is eight times higher in male smokers and nine times higher in female smokers than in nonsmokers.

Today I feel:

_____
_____
_____

Plan C
One-Pack-Per-Day Addiction:
Gradual-Cessation Smoking Log

DAY 15 or DAY ___

My allotment for today is a count of 6 cigarettes, or an alternate count of _____ cigarettes.

I agree to smoke my allotment of _____ cigarettes today.

_____   _____

Today's date   My signature

"Get Real/Stay Real" thought for today:

Smoking increases the heart rate by as much as 30 percent during the first 10 minutes of smoking.

Today I feel:

_____

_____

_____

DAY 16 or DAY ___

My allotment for today is a count of 5 cigarettes, or an alternate count of _____ cigarettes.

I agree to smoke my allotment of _____ cigarettes today.

_____   _____

Today's date   My signature

"Get Real/Stay Real" thought for today:

Smokers experience an acute increase in their blood pressure; the blood vessels constrict, forcing the heart to work harder to deliver oxygen to the heart, as well as to the rest of the body.

Today I feel:

_____

_____

_____

Plan C
One-Pack-Per-Day Addiction:
Gradual-Cessation Smoking Log

DAY 17 or DAY ___

My allotment for today is a count of 4 cigarettes, or an alternate count of _____ cigarettes.

I agree to smoke my allotment of _____ cigarettes today.

_____   _____

Today's date   My signature

"Get Real/Stay Real" thought for today:
Smoking puts one at as much risk for developing arteriosclerosis as does high blood pressure and high blood cholesterol.

Today I feel:

_____

_____

_____

DAY 18 or DAY ___

My allotment for today is a count of 3 cigarettes, or an alternate count of _____ cigarettes.

I agree to smoke my allotment of _____ cigarettes today.

_____   _____

Today's date   My signature

"Get Real/Stay Real" thought for today:
Although doctors often prescribe aspirin to help prevent clot formation that can cause heart disease, aspirin is less effective for smokers.

Today I feel:

_____

_____

_____

Plan C
One-Pack-Per-Day Addiction:
Gradual-Cessation Smoking Log

DAY 19 or DAY ___

My allotment for today is a count of 2 cigarettes, or an alternate count of _____ cigarettes.

I agree to smoke my allotment of _____ cigarettes today.

_____   _____
Today's date   My signature

"Get Real/Stay Real" thought for today:
Smoking causes higher levels of free fatty acids in the bloodstream, raising levels of LDL, or bad cholesterol, and lowering levels of HDL, or good cholesterol.

Today I feel:

_____
_____
_____

DAY 20 or DAY ___   <u>FINAL DAY</u>

My allotment for today is a count of 1 cigarette. An alternate count of _____ cigarettes.

I agree to smoke my allotment of _____ cigarettes today.

_____   _____
Today's date   My signature

"Get Real/Stay Real" thought for today:
Women smokers experience earlier menopause, raising heart-disease risk. Even women smokers who have not yet reached menopause have lower-than-normal estrogen levels, increasing their heart-disease risk.

Plan C
One-Pack-Per-Day Addiction:
Gradual-Cessation Smoking Log

Congratulations! You have successfully completed
your smoking-cessation program!
Now, turn to page 141 to begin the first 90 days of
your new *smoke-free* life!

Your First 90 Days
Smoke-Free Log

Welcome to the first 90 days of your new smoke-free life. *Congratulations* on your continuing efforts and best wishes to you as you join countless thousands of new smoke-free friends who would also congratulate and support you, if they could be here today.

Allow me to encourage you by way of the printed page to congratulate yourself and credit yourself for your magnificent achievement!

Addiction is slavery. To escape from the slavery of addiction is to experience a refound freedom. Life, to be sure, has its bumps and grinds, but nicotine addiction, in reality, only *exacerbates* said bumps and grinds.

I encourage you to enjoy your first smoke-free day—this very special moment in your life—acknowledging it in a way you feel appropriate. Perhaps you'll be private about it, perhaps you'll share it with others.

And thanks also for contributing to a healthier, happier environment!

Your First 90 Days
—Smoke-Free Log—

DAY 1   MORNING
Today I celebrate myself and my achievement. I look into my mirror and say what I feel:

_____

_____

_____

DAY 1   BEDTIME
Today has been the first day of my new smoke-free life. I look into my mirror and say what I feel:

_____

_____

_____

_____

_____   _____
Today's date   My signature

DAY 2   MORNING
Today I celebrate myself and my achievement. I look into my mirror and say what I feel:

_____

_____

_____

DAY 2   BEDTIME
Today has been the second day of my new smoke-free life. I look into my mirror and say what I feel:

_____

_____

_____

_____

_____   _____
Today's date   My signature

Your First 90 Days
—Smoke-Free Log—

DAY 3   MORNING

Today I celebrate myself and my achievement. I look into my mirror and say what I feel:

_____

_____

_____

DAY 3   BEDTIME

Today has been the third day of my new smoke-free life. I look into my mirror and say what I feel:

_____

_____

_____

_____

_____   _____

Today's date   My signature

DAY 4   MORNING

Today I celebrate myself and my achievement. I look into my mirror and say what I feel:

_____

_____

_____

DAY 4   BEDTIME

Today has been the fourth day of my new smoke-free life. I look into my mirror and say what I feel:

_____

_____

_____

_____

_____   _____

Today's date   My signature

Your First 90 Days
—Smoke-Free Log—

DAY 5   MORNING
Today I celebrate myself and my achievement. I look into my mirror and say what I feel:

_____

_____

_____

DAY 5   BEDTIME
Today has been the fifth day of my new smoke-free life. I look into my mirror and say what I feel:

_____

_____

_____

_____

_____   _____

Today's date   My signature

DAY 6   MORNING
Today I celebrate myself and my achievement. I look into my mirror and say what I feel:

_____

_____

_____

DAY 6   BEDTIME
Today has been the sixth day of my new smoke-free life. I look into my mirror and say what I feel:

_____

_____

_____

_____

_____   _____

Today's date   My signature

Your First 90 Days
—Smoke-Free Log—

DAY 7   MORNING
Today I celebrate myself and my achievement. I look into my mirror and say what I feel:

_____

_____

_____

DAY 7   BEDTIME
Today has been the seventh day of my new smoke-free life. I look into my mirror and say what I feel:

_____

_____

_____

_____

_____   _____
Today's date   My signature

DAY 8   MORNING
Today I celebrate myself and my achievement. I look into my mirror and say what I feel:

_____

_____

_____

DAY 8   BEDTIME
Today has been the eighth day of my new smoke-free life. I look into my mirror and say what I feel:

_____

_____

_____

_____

_____   _____
Today's date   My signature

Your First 90 Days
—Smoke-Free Log—

DAY 9   MORNING
Today I celebrate myself and my achievement. I look into my mirror and say what I feel:

_____
_____
_____

DAY 9   BEDTIME
Today has been the ninth day of my new smoke-free life. I look into my mirror and say what I feel:

_____
_____
_____
_____

_____   _____
Today's date   My signature

DAY 10   MORNING
Today I celebrate myself and my achievement. I look into my mirror and say what I feel:

_____
_____
_____

DAY 10   BEDTIME
Today has been the tenth day of my new smoke-free life. I look into my mirror and say what I feel:

_____
_____
_____
_____

_____   _____
Today's date   My signature

Your First 90 Days
—Smoke-Free Log—

DAY 11   MORNING
Today I celebrate myself and my achievement. I look into my mirror and say what I feel:

_____

_____

_____

DAY 11   BEDTIME
Today has been the eleventh day of my new smoke-free life. I look into my mirror and say what I feel:

_____

_____

_____

_____

_____   _____

Today's date   My signature

DAY 12   MORNING
Today I celebrate myself and my achievement. I look into my mirror and say what I feel:

_____

_____

_____

DAY 12   BEDTIME
Today has been the twelfth day of my new smoke-free life. I look into my mirror and say what I feel:

_____

_____

_____

_____

_____   _____

Today's date   My signature

Your First 90 Days
—Smoke-Free Log—

DAY 13   MORNING
Today I celebrate myself and my achievement. I look into my mirror and say what I feel:

_____
_____
_____

DAY 13   BEDTIME
Today has been the thirteenth day of my new smoke-free life. I look into my mirror and say what I feel:

_____
_____
_____
_____

_____   _____
Today's date   My signature

DAY 14   MORNING
Today I celebrate myself and my achievement. I look into my mirror and say what I feel:

_____
_____
_____

DAY 14   BEDTIME
Today has been the fourteenth day of my new smoke-free life. I look into my mirror and say what I feel:

_____
_____
_____
_____

_____   _____
Today's date   My signature

Your First 90 Days
—Smoke-Free Log—

DAY 15   MORNING
Today I celebrate myself and my achievement. I look into my mirror
and say what I feel:

_____

_____

_____

DAY 15   BEDTIME
Today has been the fifteenth day of my new smoke-free life. I look
into my mirror and say what I feel:

_____

_____

_____

_____

_____   _____

Today's date   My signature

DAY 16   MORNING
Today I celebrate myself and my achievement. I look into my mirror
and say what I feel:

_____

_____

_____

DAY 16   BEDTIME
Today has been the sixteenth day of my new smoke-free life. I look
into my mirror and say what I feel:

_____

_____

_____

_____

_____   _____

Today's date   My signature

Your First 90 Days
—Smoke-Free Log—

DAY 17   MORNING
Today I celebrate myself and my achievement. I look into my mirror and say what I feel:

_____
_____
_____

DAY 17   BEDTIME
Today has been the seventeenth day of my new smoke-free life. I look into my mirror and say what I feel:

_____
_____
_____
_____

_____   _____
Today's date   My signature

DAY 18   MORNING
Today I celebrate myself and my achievement. I look into my mirror and say what I feel:

_____
_____
_____

DAY 18   BEDTIME
Today has been the eighteenth day of my new smoke-free life. I look into my mirror and say what I feel:

_____
_____
_____
_____

_____   _____
Today's date   My signature

Your First 90 Days
—Smoke-Free Log—

DAY 19   MORNING
Today I celebrate myself and my achievement. I look into my mirror
and say what I feel:

_____

_____

_____

DAY 19   BEDTIME
Today has been the nineteenth day of my new smoke-free life. I look
into my mirror and say what I feel:

_____

_____

_____

_____

_____   _____
Today's date   My signature

DAY 20   MORNING
Today I celebrate myself and my achievement. I look into my mirror
and say what I feel:

_____

_____

_____

DAY 20   BEDTIME
Today has been the twentieth day of my new smoke-free life. I look
into my mirror and say what I feel:

_____

_____

_____

_____

_____   _____
Today's date   My signature

Your First 90 Days
—Smoke-Free Log—

DAY 21   MORNING
Today I celebrate myself and my achievement. I look into my mirror
and say what I feel:

_____
_____
_____

DAY 21   BEDTIME
Today has been the twenty-first day of my new smoke-free life. I
look into my mirror and say what I feel:

_____
_____
_____
_____

_____   _____
Today's date   My signature

DAY 22   MORNING
Today I celebrate myself and my achievement. I look into my mirror
and say what I feel:

_____
_____
_____

DAY 22   BEDTIME
Today has been the twenty-second day of my new smoke-free life. I
look into my mirror and say what I feel:

_____
_____
_____
_____

_____   _____
Today's date   My signature

Your First 90 Days
—Smoke-Free Log—

DAY 23   MORNING
Today I celebrate myself and my achievement. I look into my mirror and say what I feel:

_____

_____

_____

DAY 23   BEDTIME
Today has been the twenty-third day of my new smoke-free life. I look into my mirror and say what I feel:

_____

_____

_____

_____

_____   _____
Today's date   My signature

DAY 24   MORNING
Today I celebrate myself and my achievement. I look into my mirror and say what I feel:

_____

_____

_____

DAY 24   BEDTIME
Today has been the twenty-fourth day of my new smoke-free life. I look into my mirror and say what I feel:

_____

_____

_____

_____

_____   _____
Today's date   My signature

Your First 90 Days
—Smoke-Free Log—

DAY 25   MORNING
Today I celebrate myself and my achievement. I look into my mirror and say what I feel:

_____
_____
_____

DAY 25   BEDTIME
Today has been the twenty-fifth day of my new smoke-free life. I look into my mirror and say what I feel:

_____
_____
_____
_____

_____   _____
Today's date   My signature

DAY 26   MORNING
Today I celebrate myself and my achievement. I look into my mirror and say what I feel:

_____
_____
_____

DAY 26   BEDTIME
Today has been the twenty-sixth day of my new smoke-free life. I look into my mirror and say what I feel:

_____
_____
_____
_____

_____   _____
Today's date   My signature

Your First 90 Days
—Smoke-Free Log—

DAY 27   MORNING

Today I celebrate myself and my achievement. I look into my mirror and say what I feel:

_____

_____

_____

DAY 27   BEDTIME

Today has been the twenty-seventh day of my new smoke-free life. I look into my mirror and say what I feel:

_____

_____

_____

_____

_____   _____

Today's date   My signature

DAY 28   MORNING

Today I celebrate myself and my achievement. I look into my mirror and say what I feel:

_____

_____

_____

DAY 28   BEDTIME

Today has been the twenty-eighth day of my new smoke-free life. I look into my mirror and say what I feel:

_____

_____

_____

_____

_____   _____

Today's date   My signature

Your First 90 Days
—Smoke-Free Log—

DAY 29   MORNING

Today I celebrate myself and my achievement. I look into my mirror and say what I feel:

_____

_____

_____

DAY 29   BEDTIME

Today has been the twenty-ninth day of my new smoke-free life. I look into my mirror and say what I feel:

_____

_____

_____

_____

_____   _____

Today's date   My signature

DAY 30   MORNING

Today I celebrate myself and my achievement. I look into my mirror and say what I feel:

_____

_____

_____

DAY 30   BEDTIME

Today has been the thirtieth day of my new smoke-free life. I look into my mirror and say what I feel:

_____

_____

_____

_____

_____   _____

Today's date   My signature

Your First 90 Days
—Smoke-Free Log—

DAY 31   MORNING
Today I celebrate myself and my achievement. I look into my mirror and say what I feel:

_____

_____

_____

DAY 31   BEDTIME
Today has been the thirty-first day of my new smoke-free life. I look into my mirror and say what I feel:

_____

_____

_____

_____

_____   _____

Today's date   My signature

DAY 32   MORNING
Today I celebrate myself and my achievement. I look into my mirror and say what I feel:

_____

_____

_____

DAY 32   BEDTIME
Today has been the thirty-second day of my new smoke-free life. I look into my mirror and say what I feel:

_____

_____

_____

_____

_____   _____

Today's date   My signature

Your First 90 Days
—Smoke-Free Log—

DAY 33   MORNING
Today I celebrate myself and my achievement. I look into my mirror
and say what I feel:

_____

_____

_____

DAY 33   BEDTIME
Today has been the thirty-third day of my new smoke-free life. I look
into my mirror and say what I feel:

_____

_____

_____

_____

_____   _____

Today's date   My signature

DAY 34   MORNING
Today I celebrate myself and my achievement. I look into my mirror
and say what I feel:

_____

_____

_____

DAY 34   BEDTIME
Today has been the thirty-fourth day of my new smoke-free life. I
look into my mirror and say what I feel:

_____

_____

_____

_____

_____   _____

Today's date   My signature

Your First 90 Days
—Smoke-Free Log—

DAY 35   MORNING
Today I celebrate myself and my achievement. I look into my mirror and say what I feel:

_____

_____

_____

DAY 35   BEDTIME
Today has been the thirty-fifth day of my new smoke-free life. I look into my mirror and say what I feel:

_____

_____

_____

_____

_____   _____

Today's date   My signature

DAY 36   MORNING
Today I celebrate myself and my achievement. I look into my mirror and say what I feel:

_____

_____

_____

DAY 36   BEDTIME
Today has been the thirty-sixth day of my new smoke-free life. I look into my mirror and say what I feel:

_____

_____

_____

_____

_____   _____

Today's date   My signature

Your First 90 Days
—Smoke-Free Log—

DAY 37   MORNING
Today I celebrate myself and my achievement. I look into my mirror and say what I feel:

_____

_____

_____

DAY 37   BEDTIME
Today has been the thirty-seventh day of my new smoke-free life. I look into my mirror and say what I feel:

_____

_____

_____

_____

_____   _____
Today's date   My signature

DAY 38   MORNING
Today I celebrate myself and my achievement. I look into my mirror and say what I feel:

_____

_____

_____

DAY 38   BEDTIME
Today has been the thirty-eighth day of my new smoke-free life. I look into my mirror and say what I feel:

_____

_____

_____

_____

_____   _____
Today's date   My signature

Your First 90 Days
—Smoke-Free Log—

DAY 39   MORNING
Today I celebrate myself and my achievement. I look into my mirror and say what I feel:

_____

_____

_____

DAY 39   BEDTIME
Today has been the thirty-ninth day of my new smoke-free life. I look into my mirror and say what I feel:

_____

_____

_____

_____

_____   _____

Today's date   My signature

DAY 40   MORNING
Today I celebrate myself and my achievement. I look into my mirror and say what I feel:

_____

_____

_____

DAY 40   BEDTIME
Today has been the fortieth day of my new smoke-free life. I look into my mirror and say what I feel:

_____

_____

_____

_____

_____   _____

Today's date   My signature

Your First 90 Days
—Smoke-Free Log—

DAY 41   MORNING
Today I celebrate myself and my achievement. I look into my mirror and say what I feel:

_____

_____

_____

DAY 41   BEDTIME
Today has been the forty-first day of my new smoke-free life. I look into my mirror and say what I feel:

_____

_____

_____

_____

_____   _____
Today's date   My signature

DAY 42   MORNING
Today I celebrate myself and my achievement. I look into my mirror and say what I feel:

_____

_____

_____

DAY 42   BEDTIME
Today has been the forty-second day of my new smoke-free life. I look into my mirror and say what I feel:

_____

_____

_____

_____

_____   _____
Today's date   My signature

Your First 90 Days
—Smoke-Free Log—

DAY 43   MORNING
Today I celebrate myself and my achievement. I look into my mirror and say what I feel:

_____

_____

_____

DAY 43   BEDTIME
Today has been the forty-third day of my new smoke-free life. I look into my mirror and say what I feel:

_____

_____

_____

_____

_____   _____

Today's date   My signature

DAY 44   MORNING
Today I celebrate myself and my achievement. I look into my mirror and say what I feel:

_____

_____

_____

DAY 44   BEDTIME
Today has been the forty-fourth day of my new smoke-free life. I look into my mirror and say what I feel:

_____

_____

_____

_____

_____   _____

Today's date   My signature

Your First 90 Days
—Smoke-Free Log—

DAY 45   MORNING
Today I celebrate myself and my achievement. I look into my mirror and say what I feel:

_____
_____
_____

DAY 45   BEDTIME
Today has been the forty-fifth day of my new smoke-free life. I look into my mirror and say what I feel:

_____
_____
_____
_____

_____   _____
Today's date   My signature

DAY 46   MORNING
Today I celebrate myself and my achievement. I look into my mirror and say what I feel:

_____
_____
_____

DAY 46   BEDTIME
Today has been the forty-sixth day of my new smoke-free life. I look into my mirror and say what I feel:

_____
_____
_____
_____

_____   _____
Today's date   My signature

Your First 90 Days
—Smoke-Free Log—

DAY 47   MORNING
Today I celebrate myself and my achievement. I look into my mirror and say what I feel:

_____

_____

_____

DAY 47   BEDTIME
Today has been the forty-seventh day of my new smoke-free life. I look into my mirror and say what I feel:

_____

_____

_____

_____

_____   _____
Today's date   My signature

DAY 48   MORNING
Today I celebrate myself and my achievement. I look into my mirror and say what I feel:

_____

_____

_____

DAY 48   BEDTIME
Today has been the forty-eighth day of my new smoke-free life. I look into my mirror and say what I feel:

_____

_____

_____

_____

_____   _____
Today's date   My signature

Your First 90 Days
—Smoke-Free Log—

DAY 49   MORNING
Today I celebrate myself and my achievement. I look into my mirror and say what I feel:

_____

_____

_____

DAY 49   BEDTIME
Today has been the forty-ninth day of my new smoke-free life. I look into my mirror and say what I feel:

_____

_____

_____

_____

_____   _____
Today's date   My signature

DAY 50   MORNING
Today I celebrate myself and my achievement. I look into my mirror and say what I feel:

_____

_____

_____

DAY 50   BEDTIME
Today has been the fiftieth day of my new smoke-free life. I look into my mirror and say what I feel:

_____

_____

_____

_____

_____   _____
Today's date   My signature

Your First 90 Days
—Smoke-Free Log—

DAY 51   MORNING

Today I celebrate myself and my achievement. I look into my mirror and say what I feel:

_____

_____

_____

DAY 51   BEDTIME

Today has been the fifty-first day of my new smoke-free life. I look into my mirror and say what I feel:

_____

_____

_____

_____

_____   _____
Today's date   My signature

DAY 52   MORNING

Today I celebrate myself and my achievement. I look into my mirror and say what I feel:

_____

_____

_____

DAY 52   BEDTIME

Today has been the fifty-second day of my new smoke-free life. I look into my mirror and say what I feel:

_____

_____

_____

_____

_____   _____
Today's date   My signature

Your First 90 Days
—Smoke-Free Log—

DAY 53   MORNING

Today I celebrate myself and my achievement. I look into my mirror and say what I feel:

_____
_____
_____

DAY 53   BEDTIME

Today has been the fifty-third day of my new smoke-free life. I look into my mirror and say what I feel:

_____
_____
_____
_____

_____   _____

Today's date   My signature

DAY 54   MORNING

Today I celebrate myself and my achievement. I look into my mirror and say what I feel:

_____
_____
_____

DAY 54   BEDTIME

Today has been the fifty-fourth day of my new smoke-free life. I look into my mirror and say what I feel:

_____
_____
_____
_____

_____   _____

Today's date   My signature

Your First 90 Days
—Smoke-Free Log—

DAY 55   MORNING
Today I celebrate myself and my achievement. I look into my mirror and say what I feel:

_____
_____
_____

DAY 55   BEDTIME
Today has been the fifty-fifth day of my new smoke-free life. I look into my mirror and say what I feel:

_____
_____
_____
_____

_____   _____
Today's date   My signature

DAY 56   MORNING
Today I celebrate myself and my achievement. I look into my mirror and say what I feel:

_____
_____
_____

DAY 56   BEDTIME
Today has been the fifty-sixth day of my new smoke-free life. I look into my mirror and say what I feel:

_____
_____
_____
_____

_____   _____
Today's date   My signature

Your First 90 Days
—Smoke-Free Log—

DAY 57   MORNING
Today I celebrate myself and my achievement. I look into my mirror and say what I feel:

_____

_____

_____

DAY 57   BEDTIME
Today has been the fifty-seventh day of my new smoke-free life. I look into my mirror and say what I feel:

_____

_____

_____

_____

_____   _____
Today's date   My signature

DAY 58   MORNING
Today I celebrate myself and my achievement. I look into my mirror and say what I feel:

_____

_____

_____

DAY 58   BEDTIME
Today has been the fifty-eighth day of my new smoke-free life. I look into my mirror and say what I feel:

_____

_____

_____

_____

_____   _____
Today's date   My signature

Your First 90 Days
—Smoke-Free Log—

DAY 59   MORNING
Today I celebrate myself and my achievement. I look into my mirror and say what I feel:

_____
_____
_____

DAY 59   BEDTIME
Today has been the fifty-ninth day of my new smoke-free life. I look into my mirror and say what I feel:

_____
_____
_____
_____

_____   _____
Today's date   My signature

DAY 60   MORNING
Today I celebrate myself and my achievement. I look into my mirror and say what I feel:

_____
_____
_____

DAY 60   BEDTIME
Today has been the sixtieth day of my new smoke-free life. I look into my mirror and say what I feel:

_____
_____
_____
_____

_____   _____
Today's date   My signature

Your First 90 Days
—Smoke-Free Log—

DAY 61   MORNING
Today I celebrate myself and my achievement. I look into my mirror and say what I feel:

_____
_____
_____

DAY 61   BEDTIME
Today has been the sixty-first day of my new smoke-free life. I look into my mirror and say what I feel:

_____
_____
_____
_____

_____   _____
Today's date   My signature

DAY 62   MORNING
Today I celebrate myself and my achievement. I look into my mirror and say what I feel:

_____
_____
_____

DAY 62   BEDTIME
Today has been the sixty-second day of my new smoke-free life. I look into my mirror and say what I feel:

_____
_____
_____
_____

_____   _____
Today's date   My signature

Your First 90 Days
—Smoke-Free Log—

DAY 63   MORNING

Today I celebrate myself and my achievement. I look into my mirror and say what I feel:

_____

_____

_____

DAY 63   BEDTIME

Today has been the sixty-third day of my new smoke-free life. I look into my mirror and say what I feel:

_____

_____

_____

_____

_____   _____

Today's date   My signature

DAY 64   MORNING

Today I celebrate myself and my achievement. I look into my mirror and say what I feel:

_____

_____

_____

DAY 64   BEDTIME

Today has been the sixty-fourth day of my new smoke-free life. I look into my mirror and say what I feel:

_____

_____

_____

_____

_____   _____

Today's date   My signature

Your First 90 Days
—Smoke-Free Log—

DAY 65   MORNING
Today I celebrate myself and my achievement. I look into my mirror and say what I feel:

_____

_____

_____

DAY 65   BEDTIME
Today has been the sixty-fifth day of my new smoke-free life. I look into my mirror and say what I feel:

_____

_____

_____

_____

_____   _____
Today's date   My signature

DAY 66   MORNING
Today I celebrate myself and my achievement. I look into my mirror and say what I feel:

_____

_____

_____

DAY 66   BEDTIME
Today has been the sixty-sixth day of my new smoke-free life. I look into my mirror and say what I feel:

_____

_____

_____

_____

_____   _____
Today's date   My signature

Your First 90 Days
—Smoke-Free Log—

DAY 67   MORNING
Today I celebrate myself and my achievement. I look into my mirror and say what I feel:

_____

_____

_____

DAY 67   BEDTIME
Today has been the sixty-seventh day of my new smoke-free life. I look into my mirror and say what I feel:

_____

_____

_____

_____

_____   _____
Today's date   My signature

DAY 68   MORNING
Today I celebrate myself and my achievement. I look into my mirror and say what I feel:

_____

_____

_____

DAY 68   BEDTIME
Today has been the sixty-eighth day of my new smoke-free life. I look into my mirror and say what I feel:

_____

_____

_____

_____

_____   _____
Today's date   My signature

Your First 90 Days
—Smoke-Free Log—

DAY 69 MORNING
Today I celebrate myself and my achievement. I look into my mirror and say what I feel:

_____
_____
_____

DAY 69 BEDTIME
Today has been the sixty-ninth day of my new smoke-free life. I look into my mirror and say what I feel:

_____
_____
_____
_____

_____   _____
Today's date   My signature

DAY 70 MORNING
Today I celebrate myself and my achievement. I look into my mirror and say what I feel:

_____
_____
_____

DAY 70 BEDTIME
Today has been the seventieth day of my new smoke-free life. I look into my mirror and say what I feel:

_____
_____
_____
_____

_____   _____
Today's date   My signature

Your First 90 Days
—Smoke-Free Log—

DAY 71   MORNING
Today I celebrate myself and my achievement. I look into my mirror and say what I feel:

_____

_____

_____

DAY 71   BEDTIME
Today has been the seventy-first day of my new smoke-free life. I look into my mirror and say what I feel:

_____

_____

_____

_____

_____

Today's date   My signature

DAY 72   MORNING
Today I celebrate myself and my achievement. I look into my mirror and say what I feel:

_____

_____

_____

DAY 72   BEDTIME
Today has been the seventy-second day of my new smoke-free life. I look into my mirror and say what I feel:

_____

_____

_____

_____

_____

Today's date   My signature

Your First 90 Days
—Smoke-Free Log—

DAY 73   MORNING
Today I celebrate myself and my achievement. I look into my mirror and say what I feel:

_____

_____

_____

DAY 73   BEDTIME
Today has been the seventy-third day of my new smoke-free life. I look into my mirror and say what I feel:

_____

_____

_____

_____

_____   _____

Today's date   My signature

DAY 74   MORNING
Today I celebrate myself and my achievement. I look into my mirror and say what I feel:

_____

_____

_____

DAY 74   BEDTIME
Today has been the seventy-fourth day of my new smoke-free life. I look into my mirror and say what I feel:

_____

_____

_____

_____

_____   _____

Today's date   My signature

Your First 90 Days
—Smoke-Free Log—

DAY 75   MORNING
Today I celebrate myself and my achievement. I look into my mirror and say what I feel:

_____

_____

_____

DAY 75   BEDTIME
Today has been the seventy-fifth day of my new smoke-free life. I look into my mirror and say what I feel:

_____

_____

_____

_____

_____   _____

Today's date   My signature

DAY 76   MORNING
Today I celebrate myself and my achievement. I look into my mirror and say what I feel:

_____

_____

_____

DAY 76   BEDTIME
Today has been the seventy-sixth day of my new smoke-free life. I look into my mirror and say what I feel:

_____

_____

_____

_____

_____   _____

Today's date   My signature

Your First 90 Days
—Smoke-Free Log—

DAY 77   MORNING
Today I celebrate myself and my achievement. I look into my mirror and say what I feel:

_____

_____

_____

DAY 77   BEDTIME
Today has been the seventy-seventh day of my new smoke-free life. I look into my mirror and say what I feel:

_____

_____

_____

_____

_____   _____
Today's date   My signature

DAY 78   MORNING
Today I celebrate myself and my achievement. I look into my mirror and say what I feel:

_____

_____

_____

DAY 78   BEDTIME
Today has been the seventy-eighth day of my new smoke-free life. I look into my mirror and say what I feel:

_____

_____

_____

_____

_____   _____
Today's date   My signature

Your First 90 Days
—Smoke-Free Log—

DAY 79   MORNING
Today I celebrate myself and my achievement. I look into my mirror and say what I feel:

_____

_____

_____

DAY 79   BEDTIME
Today has been the seventy-ninth day of my new smoke-free life. I look into my mirror and say what I feel:

_____

_____

_____

_____

_____   _____

Today's date   My signature

DAY 80   MORNING
Today I celebrate myself and my achievement. I look into my mirror and say what I feel:

_____

_____

_____

DAY 80   BEDTIME
Today has been the eightieth day of my new smoke-free life. I look into my mirror and say what I feel:

_____

_____

_____

_____

_____   _____

Today's date   My signature

Your First 90 Days
—Smoke-Free Log—

DAY 81   MORNING
Today I celebrate myself and my achievement. I look into my mirror and say what I feel:

_____

_____

_____

DAY 81   BEDTIME
Today has been the eighty-first day of my new smoke-free life. I look into my mirror and say what I feel:

_____

_____

_____

_____

_____   _____

Today's date   My signature

DAY 82   MORNING
Today I celebrate myself and my achievement. I look into my mirror and say what I feel:

_____

_____

_____

DAY 82   BEDTIME
Today has been the eighty-second day of my new smoke-free life. I look into my mirror and say what I feel:

_____

_____

_____

_____

_____   _____

Today's date   My signature

Your First 90 Days
—Smoke-Free Log—

DAY 83   MORNING
Today I celebrate myself and my achievement. I look into my mirror and say what I feel:

_____

_____

_____

DAY 83   BEDTIME
Today has been the eighty-third day of my new smoke-free life. I look into my mirror and say what I feel:

_____

_____

_____

_____

_____   _____
Today's date   My signature

DAY 84   MORNING
Today I celebrate myself and my achievement. I look into my mirror and say what I feel:

_____

_____

_____

DAY 84   BEDTIME
Today has been the eighty-fourth day of my new smoke-free life. I look into my mirror and say what I feel:

_____

_____

_____

_____

_____   _____
Today's date   My signature

Your First 90 Days
—Smoke-Free Log—

DAY 85   MORNING
Today I celebrate myself and my achievement. I look into my mirror and say what I feel:

_____

_____

_____

DAY 85   BEDTIME
Today has been the eighty-fifth day of my new smoke-free life. I look into my mirror and say what I feel:

_____

_____

_____

_____

_____   _____
Today's date   My signature

DAY 86   MORNING
Today I celebrate myself and my achievement. I look into my mirror and say what I feel:

_____

_____

_____

DAY 86   BEDTIME
Today has been the eighty-sixth day of my new smoke-free life. I look into my mirror and say what I feel:

_____

_____

_____

_____

_____   _____
Today's date   My signature

Your First 90 Days
—Smoke-Free Log—

DAY 87   MORNING
Today I celebrate myself and my achievement. I look into my mirror and say what I feel:

_____

_____

_____

DAY 87   BEDTIME
Today has been the eighty-seventh day of my new smoke-free life. I look into my mirror and say what I feel:

_____

_____

_____

_____

_____   _____

Today's date   My signature

DAY 88   MORNING
Today I celebrate myself and my achievement. I look into my mirror and say what I feel:

_____

_____

_____

DAY 88   BEDTIME
Today has been the eighty-eighth day of my new smoke-free life. I look into my mirror and say what I feel:

_____

_____

_____

_____

_____   _____

Today's date   My signature

Your First 90 Days
—Smoke-Free Log—

DAY 89   MORNING
Today I celebrate myself and my achievement. I look into my mirror and say what I feel:

_____

_____

_____

DAY 89   BEDTIME
Today has been the eighty-ninth day of my new smoke-free life. I look into my mirror and say what I feel:

_____

_____

_____

_____

_____   _____

Today's date   My signature

DAY 90   MORNING
Today I celebrate myself and my achievement. I look into my mirror and say what I feel:

_____

_____

_____

DAY 90   BEDTIME
Today has been the ninetieth day of my new smoke-free life. I look into my mirror and say what I feel:

_____

_____

_____

_____

_____   _____

Today's date   My signature

Congratulations on your first 90 days of a smoke-free life. Keep your nicotine addiction arrested and *continue* to build your new life by keeping nicotine out of your system *no matter what*!

Continue to acknowledge each new smoke-free day in the log that follows.

Again, congratulations and all best wishes to you!

Continue to Build . . .
Your First Year
Smoke-Free Log

Isn't this great?! I'll bet you're beginning to enjoy some of the advantages of a smoke-free lifestyle by this time in your recovery. As you continue to build your first year of freedom from nicotine addiction, check out chapter 10 for a treasure trove of tobacco-free life-activity suggestions. I really wish that I could be there to give you a big, warm hug in celebration of your continuing triumph over slavery! The printed page will, however, have to suffice. Again, best wishes to you!

Continue to Build . . .
Your First Year
—Smoke-Free Log—

DAY 91   MORNING

Today I celebrate myself and my achievement. I look into my mirror and say what I feel:

_____

_____

_____

DAY 91   BEDTIME

Today has been the ninety-first day of my new smoke-free life. I look into my mirror and say what I feel:

_____

_____

_____

_____

_____   _____

Today's date   My signature

DAY 92   MORNING

Today I celebrate myself and my achievement. I look into my mirror and say what I feel:

_____

_____

_____

DAY 92   BEDTIME

Today has been the ninety-second day of my new smoke-free life. I look into my mirror and say what I feel:

_____

_____

_____

_____

_____   _____

Today's date   My signature

Continue to Build . . .
Your First Year
—Smoke-Free Log—

DAY 93   MORNING

Today I celebrate myself and my achievement. I look into my mirror and say what I feel:

_____

_____

_____

DAY 93   BEDTIME

Today has been the ninety-third day of my new smoke-free life. I look into my mirror and say what I feel:

_____

_____

_____

_____

_____   _____

Today's date   My signature

DAY 94   MORNING

Today I celebrate myself and my achievement. I look into my mirror and say what I feel:

_____

_____

_____

DAY 94   BEDTIME

Today has been the ninety-fourth day of my new smoke-free life. I look into my mirror and say what I feel:

_____

_____

_____

_____

_____   _____

Today's date   My signature

Continue to Build . . .
Your First Year
—Smoke-Free Log—

DAY 95   MORNING
Today I celebrate myself and my achievement. I look into my mirror and say what I feel:

_____

_____

_____

DAY 95   BEDTIME
Today has been the ninety-fifth day of my new smoke-free life. I look into my mirror and say what I feel:

_____

_____

_____

_____

_____   _____
Today's date   My signature

DAY 96   MORNING
Today I celebrate myself and my achievement. I look into my mirror and say what I feel:

_____

_____

_____

DAY 96   BEDTIME
Today has been the ninety-sixth day of my new smoke-free life. I look into my mirror and say what I feel:

_____

_____

_____

_____

_____   _____
Today's date   My signature

Continue to Build . . .
Your First Year
—Smoke-Free Log—

DAY 97   MORNING

Today I celebrate myself and my achievement. I look into my mirror and say what I feel:

_____

_____

_____

DAY 97   BEDTIME

Today has been the ninety-seventh day of my new smoke-free life. I look into my mirror and say what I feel:

_____

_____

_____

_____

_____   _____

Today's date   My signature

DAY 98   MORNING

Today I celebrate myself and my achievement. I look into my mirror and say what I feel:

_____

_____

_____

DAY 98   BEDTIME

Today has been the ninety-eighth day of my new smoke-free life. I look into my mirror and say what I feel:

_____

_____

_____

_____

_____   _____

Today's date   My signature

Continue to Build . . .
Your First Year
—Smoke-Free Log—

DAY 99   MORNING
Today I celebrate myself and my achievement. I look into my mirror and say what I feel:

_____

_____

_____

DAY 99   BEDTIME
Today has been the ninety-ninth day of my new smoke-free life. I look into my mirror and say what I feel:

_____

_____

_____

_____

_____   _____

Today's date   My signature

DAY 100   MORNING
Today I celebrate myself and my achievement. I look into my mirror and say what I feel:

_____

_____

_____

DAY 100   BEDTIME
Today has been the hundredth day of my new smoke-free life. I look into my mirror and say what I feel:

_____

_____

_____

_____

_____   _____

Today's date   My signature

Continue to Build . . .
Your First Year
—Smoke-Free Log—

DAY 101   MORNING

Today I celebrate myself and my achievement. I look into my mirror and say what I feel:

_____
_____
_____

DAY 101   BEDTIME

Today has been the hundred-first day of my new smoke-free life. I look into my mirror and say what I feel:

_____
_____
_____
_____

_____   _____
Today's date   My signature

DAY 102   MORNING

Today I celebrate myself and my achievement. I look into my mirror and say what I feel:

_____
_____
_____

DAY 102   BEDTIME

Today has been the hundred-second day of my new smoke-free life. I look into my mirror and say what I feel:

_____
_____
_____
_____

_____   _____
Today's date   My signature

Continue to Build . . .
Your First Year
—Smoke-Free Log—

DAY 103   MORNING

Today I celebrate myself and my achievement. I look into my mirror
and say what I feel:

_____

_____

_____

DAY 103   BEDTIME

Today has been the hundred-third day of my new smoke-free life. I
look into my mirror and say what I feel:

_____

_____

_____

_____

_____   _____

Today's date   My signature

DAY 104   MORNING

Today I celebrate myself and my achievement. I look into my mirror
and say what I feel:

_____

_____

_____

DAY 104   BEDTIME

Today has been the hundred-fourth day of my new smoke-free life. I
look into my mirror and say what I feel:

_____

_____

_____

_____

_____   _____

Today's date   My signature

Continue to Build . . .
Your First Year
—Smoke-Free Log—

DAY 105   MORNING
Today I celebrate myself and my achievement. I look into my mirror and say what I feel:

_____
_____
_____

DAY 105   BEDTIME
Today has been the hundred-fifth day of my new smoke-free life. I look into my mirror and say what I feel:

_____
_____
_____
_____

_____   _____
Today's date   My signature

DAY 106   MORNING
Today I celebrate myself and my achievement. I look into my mirror and say what I feel:

_____
_____
_____

DAY 106   BEDTIME
Today has been the hundred-sixth day of my new smoke-free life. I look into my mirror and say what I feel:

_____
_____
_____
_____

_____   _____
Today's date   My signature

Continue to Build . . .
Your First Year
—Smoke-Free Log—

DAY 107   MORNING
Today I celebrate myself and my achievement. I look into my mirror and say what I feel:

_____

_____

_____

DAY 107   BEDTIME
Today has been the hundred-seventh day of my new smoke-free life. I look into my mirror and say what I feel:

_____

_____

_____

_____

_____   _____

Today's date   My signature

DAY 108   MORNING
Today I celebrate myself and my achievement. I look into my mirror and say what I feel:

_____

_____

_____

DAY 108   BEDTIME
Today has been the hundred-eighth day of my new smoke-free life. I look into my mirror and say what I feel:

_____

_____

_____

_____

_____   _____

Today's date   My signature

Continue to Build...
Your First Year
—Smoke-Free Log—

DAY 109   MORNING
Today I celebrate myself and my achievement. I look into my mirror and say what I feel:

_____

_____

_____

DAY 109   BEDTIME
Today has been the hundred-ninth day of my new smoke-free life. I look into my mirror and say what I feel:

_____

_____

_____

_____

_____   _____
Today's date   My signature

DAY 110   MORNING
Today I celebrate myself and my achievement. I look into my mirror and say what I feel:

_____

_____

_____

DAY 110   BEDTIME
Today has been the hundred-tenth day of my new smoke-free life. I look into my mirror and say what I feel:

_____

_____

_____

_____

_____   _____
Today's date   My signature

Continue to Build . . .
Your First Year
—Smoke-Free Log—

DAY 111   MORNING

Today I celebrate myself and my achievement. I look into my mirror and say what I feel:

_____

_____

_____

DAY 111   BEDTIME

Today has been the hundred-eleventh day of my new smoke-free life. I look into my mirror and say what I feel:

_____

_____

_____

_____

_____   _____

Today's date   My signature

DAY 112   MORNING

Today I celebrate myself and my achievement. I look into my mirror and say what I feel:

_____

_____

_____

DAY 112   BEDTIME

Today has been the hundred-twelfth day of my new smoke-free life. I look into my mirror and say what I feel:

_____

_____

_____

_____

_____   _____

Today's date   My signature

Continue to Build . . .
Your First Year
—Smoke-Free Log—

DAY 113   MORNING
Today I celebrate myself and my achievement. I look into my mirror and say what I feel:

_____
_____
_____

DAY 113   BEDTIME
Today has been the hundred-thirteenth day of my new smoke-free life. I look into my mirror and say what I feel:

_____
_____
_____
_____

_____   _____
Today's date   My signature

DAY 114   MORNING
Today I celebrate myself and my achievement. I look into my mirror and say what I feel:

_____
_____
_____

DAY 114   BEDTIME
Today has been the hundred-fourteenth day of my new smoke-free life. I look into my mirror and say what I feel:

_____
_____
_____
_____

_____   _____
Today's date   My signature

Continue to Build . . .
Your First Year
—Smoke-Free Log—

DAY 115   MORNING
Today I celebrate myself and my achievement. I look into my mirror
and say what I feel:

_____

_____

DAY 115   BEDTIME
Today has been the hundred-fifteenth day of my new smoke-free life.
I look into my mirror and say what I feel:

_____

_____

_____

_____

_____   _____

Today's date   My signature

DAY 116   MORNING
Today I celebrate myself and my achievement. I look into my mirror
and say what I feel:

_____

_____

DAY 116   BEDTIME
Today has been the hundred-sixteenth day of my new smoke-free life.
I look into my mirror and say what I feel:

_____

_____

_____

_____

_____   _____

Today's date   My signature

Continue to Build . . .
Your First Year
—Smoke-Free Log—

DAY 117   MORNING

Today I celebrate myself and my achievement. I look into my mirror and say what I feel:

_____

_____

_____

DAY 117   BEDTIME

Today has been the hundred-seventeenth day of my new smoke-free life. I look into my mirror and say what I feel:

_____

_____

_____

_____

_____   _____
Today's date   My signature

DAY 118   MORNING

Today I celebrate myself and my achievement. I look into my mirror and say what I feel:

_____

_____

_____

DAY 118   BEDTIME

Today has been the hundred-eighteenth day of my new smoke-free life. I look into my mirror and say what I feel:

_____

_____

_____

_____

_____   _____
Today's date   My signature

Continue to Build . . .
Your First Year
—Smoke-Free Log—

DAY 119   MORNING

Today I celebrate myself and my achievement. I look into my mirror and say what I feel:

_____

_____

DAY 119   BEDTIME

Today has been the hundred-nineteenth day of my new smoke-free life. I look into my mirror and say what I feel:

_____

_____

_____

_____   _____
Today's date   My signature

DAY 120   MORNING

Today I celebrate myself and my achievement. I look into my mirror and say what I feel:

_____

_____

DAY 120   BEDTIME

Today has been the hundred-twentieth day of my new smoke-free life. I look into my mirror and say what I feel:

_____

_____

_____

_____   _____
Today's date   My signature

Continue to Build . . .
Your First Year
—Smoke-Free Log—

DAY 121   MORNING
Today I celebrate myself and my achievement. I look into my mirror and say what I feel:

_____

_____

DAY 121   BEDTIME
Today has been the hundred-twenty-first day of my new smoke-free life. I look into my mirror and say what I feel:

_____

_____

_____

_____

Today's date   My signature

DAY 122   MORNING
Today I celebrate myself and my achievement. I look into my mirror and say what I feel:

_____

_____

DAY 122   BEDTIME
Today has been the hundred-twenty-second day of my new smoke-free life. I look into my mirror and say what I feel:

_____

_____

_____

_____

Today's date   My signature

Continue to Build . . .
Your First Year
—Smoke-Free Log—

DAY 123   MORNING

Today I celebrate myself and my achievement. I look into my mirror and say what I feel:

_____

_____

_____

DAY 123   BEDTIME

Today has been the hundred-twenty-third day of my new smoke-free life. I look into my mirror and say what I feel:

_____

_____

_____

_____

_____   _____
Today's date   My signature

DAY 124   MORNING

Today I celebrate myself and my achievement. I look into my mirror and say what I feel:

_____

_____

_____

DAY 124   BEDTIME

Today has been the hundred-twenty-fourth day of my new smoke-free life. I look into my mirror and say what I feel:

_____

_____

_____

_____

_____   _____
Today's date   My signature

Continue to Build . . .
Your First Year
—Smoke-Free Log—

DAY 125   MORNING

Today I celebrate myself and my achievement. I look into my mirror and say what I feel:

_____

_____

_____

DAY 125   BEDTIME

Today has been the hundred-twenty-fifth day of my new smoke-free life. I look into my mirror and say what I feel:

_____

_____

_____

_____

_____   _____
Today's date   My signature

DAY 126   MORNING

Today I celebrate myself and my achievement. I look into my mirror and say what I feel:

_____

_____

_____

DAY 126   BEDTIME

Today has been the hundred-twenty-sixth day of my new smoke-free life. I look into my mirror and say what I feel:

_____

_____

_____

_____

_____   _____
Today's date   My signature

Continue to Build . . .
Your First Year
—Smoke-Free Log—

DAY 127   MORNING

Today I celebrate myself and my achievement. I look into my mirror and say what I feel:

_____

_____

DAY 127   BEDTIME

Today has been the hundred-twenty-seventh day of my new smoke-free life. I look into my mirror and say what I feel:

_____

_____

_____

_____   _____

Today's date   My signature

DAY 128   MORNING

Today I celebrate myself and my achievement. I look into my mirror and say what I feel:

_____

_____

DAY 128   BEDTIME

Today has been the hundred-twenty-eighth day of my new smoke-free life. I look into my mirror and say what I feel:

_____

_____

_____

_____   _____

Today's date   My signature

Continue to Build . . .
Your First Year
—Smoke-Free Log—

DAY 129   MORNING

Today I celebrate myself and my achievement. I look into my mirror and say what I feel:

_____

_____

_____

DAY 129   BEDTIME

Today has been the hundred-twenty-ninth day of my new smoke-free life. I look into my mirror and say what I feel:

_____

_____

_____

_____

_____   _____

Today's date   My signature

DAY 130   MORNING

Today I celebrate myself and my achievement. I look into my mirror and say what I feel:

_____

_____

_____

DAY 130   BEDTIME

Today has been the hundred-thirtieth day of my new smoke-free life. I look into my mirror and say what I feel:

_____

_____

_____

_____

_____   _____

Today's date   My signature

Continue to Build . . .
Your First Year
—Smoke-Free Log—

DAY 131   MORNING
Today I celebrate myself and my achievement. I look into my mirror and say what I feel:

_____

_____

_____

DAY 131   BEDTIME
Today has been the hundred-thirty-first day of my new smoke-free life. I look into my mirror and say what I feel:

_____

_____

_____

_____

_____   _____
Today's date   My signature

DAY 132   MORNING
Today I celebrate myself and my achievement. I look into my mirror and say what I feel:

_____

_____

_____

DAY 132   BEDTIME
Today has been the hundred-thirty-second day of my new smoke-free life. I look into my mirror and say what I feel:

_____

_____

_____

_____

_____   _____
Today's date   My signature

Continue to Build...
Your First Year
—Smoke-Free Log—

DAY 133   MORNING

Today I celebrate myself and my achievement. I look into my mirror and say what I feel:

_____

_____

_____

DAY 133   BEDTIME

Today has been the hundred-thirty-third day of my new smoke-free life. I look into my mirror and say what I feel:

_____

_____

_____

_____

_____   _____

Today's date   My signature

DAY 134   MORNING

Today I celebrate myself and my achievement. I look into my mirror and say what I feel:

_____

_____

_____

DAY 134   BEDTIME

Today has been the hundred-thirty-fourth day of my new smoke-free life. I look into my mirror and say what I feel:

_____

_____

_____

_____

_____   _____

Today's date   My signature

Continue to Build . . .
Your First Year
—Smoke-Free Log—

DAY 135   MORNING
Today I celebrate myself and my achievement. I look into my mirror and say what I feel:

_____

_____

DAY 135   BEDTIME
Today has been the hundred-thirty-fifth day of my new smoke-free life. I look into my mirror and say what I feel:

_____

_____

_____

_____

_____   _____
Today's date   My signature

DAY 136   MORNING
Today I celebrate myself and my achievement. I look into my mirror and say what I feel:

_____

_____

DAY 136   BEDTIME
Today has been the hundred-thirty-sixth day of my new smoke-free life. I look into my mirror and say what I feel:

_____

_____

_____

_____   _____
Today's date   My signature

Continue to Build . . .
Your First Year
—Smoke-Free Log—

DAY 137   MORNING
Today I celebrate myself and my achievement. I look into my mirror and say what I feel:

_____

_____

_____

DAY 137   BEDTIME
Today has been the hundred-thirty-seventh day of my new smoke-free life. I look into my mirror and say what I feel:

_____

_____

_____

_____

_____   _____
Today's date   My signature

DAY 138   MORNING
Today I celebrate myself and my achievement. I look into my mirror and say what I feel:

_____

_____

_____

DAY 138   BEDTIME
Today has been the hundred-thirty-eighth day of my new smoke-free life. I look into my mirror and say what I feel:

_____

_____

_____

_____

_____   _____
Today's date   My signature

Continue to Build . . .
Your First Year
—Smoke-Free Log—

DAY 139   MORNING

Today I celebrate myself and my achievement. I look into my mirror and say what I feel:

_____

_____

_____

DAY 139   BEDTIME

Today has been the hundred-thirty-ninth day of my new smoke-free life. I look into my mirror and say what I feel:

_____

_____

_____

_____

_____   _____

Today's date   My signature

DAY 140   MORNING

Today I celebrate myself and my achievement. I look into my mirror and say what I feel:

_____

_____

_____

DAY 140   BEDTIME

Today has been the hundred-fortieth day of my new smoke-free life. I look into my mirror and say what I feel:

_____

_____

_____

_____

_____   _____

Today's date   My signature

Continue to Build . . .
Your First Year
—Smoke-Free Log—

DAY 141   MORNING
Today I celebrate myself and my achievement. I look into my mirror and say what I feel:

_____

_____

_____

DAY 141   BEDTIME
Today has been the hundred-forty-first day of my new smoke-free life. I look into my mirror and say what I feel:

_____

_____

_____

_____

_____   _____
Today's date   My signature

DAY 142   MORNING
Today I celebrate myself and my achievement. I look into my mirror and say what I feel:

_____

_____

_____

DAY 142   BEDTIME
Today has been the hundred-forty-second day of my new smoke-free life. I look into my mirror and say what I feel:

_____

_____

_____

_____   _____
Today's date   My signature

Continue to Build . . .
Your First Year
—Smoke-Free Log—

DAY 143   MORNING

Today I celebrate myself and my achievement. I look into my mirror and say what I feel:

_____

_____

_____

DAY 143   BEDTIME

Today has been the hundred-forty-third day of my new smoke-free life. I look into my mirror and say what I feel:

_____

_____

_____

_____

_____   _____
Today's date   My signature

DAY 144   MORNING

Today I celebrate myself and my achievement. I look into my mirror and say what I feel:

_____

_____

_____

DAY 144   BEDTIME

Today has been the hundred-forty-fourth day of my new smoke-free life. I look into my mirror and say what I feel:

_____

_____

_____

_____

_____   _____
Today's date   My signature

Continue to Build . . .
Your First Year
—Smoke-Free Log—

DAY 145   MORNING
Today I celebrate myself and my achievement. I look into my mirror and say what I feel:

_____

_____

_____

DAY 145   BEDTIME
Today has been the hundred-forty-fifth day of my new smoke-free life. I look into my mirror and say what I feel:

_____

_____

_____

_____

_____   _____
Today's date   My signature

DAY 146   MORNING
Today I celebrate myself and my achievement. I look into my mirror and say what I feel:

_____

_____

_____

DAY 146   BEDTIME
Today has been the hundred-forty-sixth day of my new smoke-free life. I look into my mirror and say what I feel:

_____

_____

_____

_____

_____   _____
Today's date   My signature

Continue to Build . . .
Your First Year
—Smoke-Free Log—

DAY 147   MORNING
Today I celebrate myself and my achievement. I look into my mirror
and say what I feel:

_____

_____

DAY 147   BEDTIME
Today has been the hundred-forty-seventh day of my new smoke-free
life. I look into my mirror and say what I feel:

_____

_____

_____

_____

_____   _____
Today's date   My signature

DAY 148   MORNING
Today I celebrate myself and my achievement. I look into my mirror
and say what I feel:

_____

_____

DAY 148   BEDTIME
Today has been the hundred-forty-eighth day of my new smoke-free
life. I look into my mirror and say what I feel:

_____

_____

_____

_____   _____
Today's date   My signature

Continue to Build . . .
Your First Year
—Smoke-Free Log—

DAY 149   MORNING
Today I celebrate myself and my achievement. I look into my mirror and say what I feel:

_____

_____

_____

DAY 149   BEDTIME
Today has been the hundred-forty-ninth day of my new smoke-free life. I look into my mirror and say what I feel:

_____

_____

_____

_____

_____   _____
Today's date   My signature

DAY 150   MORNING
Today I celebrate myself and my achievement. I look into my mirror and say what I feel:

_____

_____

_____

DAY 150   BEDTIME
Today has been the hundred-fiftieth day of my new smoke-free life. I look into my mirror and say what I feel:

_____

_____

_____

_____

_____   _____
Today's date   My signature

Continue to Build . . .
Your First Year
—Smoke-Free Log—

DAY 151 MORNING

Today I celebrate myself and my achievement. I look into my mirror and say what I feel:

_____

_____

_____

DAY 151 BEDTIME

Today has been the hundred-fifty-first day of my new smoke-free life. I look into my mirror and say what I feel:

_____

_____

_____

_____

_____ _____

Today's date My signature

DAY 152 MORNING

Today I celebrate myself and my achievement. I look into my mirror and say what I feel:

_____

_____

_____

DAY 152 BEDTIME

Today has been the hundred-fifty-second day of my new smoke-free life. I look into my mirror and say what I feel:

_____

_____

_____

_____

_____ _____

Today's date My signature

Continue to Build . . .
Your First Year
—Smoke-Free Log—

DAY 153   MORNING
Today I celebrate myself and my achievement. I look into my mirror and say what I feel:

_____

_____

_____

DAY 153   BEDTIME
Today has been the hundred-fifty-third day of my new smoke-free life. I look into my mirror and say what I feel:

_____

_____

_____

_____

_____   _____
Today's date   My signature

DAY 154   MORNING
Today I celebrate myself and my achievement. I look into my mirror and say what I feel:

_____

_____

_____

DAY 154   BEDTIME
Today has been the hundred-fifty-fourth day of my new smoke-free life. I look into my mirror and say what I feel:

_____

_____

_____

_____

_____   _____
Today's date   My signature

Continue to Build . . .
Your First Year
—Smoke-Free Log—

DAY 155   MORNING

Today I celebrate myself and my achievement. I look into my mirror and say what I feel:

_____

_____

_____

DAY 155   BEDTIME

Today has been the hundred-fifty-fifth day of my new smoke-free life. I look into my mirror and say what I feel:

_____

_____

_____

_____

_____   _____
Today's date   My signature

DAY 156   MORNING

Today I celebrate myself and my achievement. I look into my mirror and say what I feel:

_____

_____

_____

DAY 156   BEDTIME

Today has been the hundred-fifty-sixth day of my new smoke-free life. I look into my mirror and say what I feel:

_____

_____

_____

_____

_____   _____
Today's date   My signature

Continue to Build . . .
Your First Year
—Smoke-Free Log—

DAY 157   MORNING

Today I celebrate myself and my achievement. I look into my mirror and say what I feel:

_____

_____

_____

DAY 157   BEDTIME

Today has been the hundred-fifty-seventh day of my new smoke-free life. I look into my mirror and say what I feel:

_____

_____

_____

_____

_____   _____
Today's date   My signature

DAY 158   MORNING

Today I celebrate myself and my achievement. I look into my mirror and say what I feel:

_____

_____

_____

DAY 158   BEDTIME

Today has been the hundred-fifty-eighth day of my new smoke-free life. I look into my mirror and say what I feel:

_____

_____

_____

_____

_____   _____
Today's date   My signature

Continue to Build . . .
Your First Year
—Smoke-Free Log—

DAY 159   MORNING

Today I celebrate myself and my achievement. I look into my mirror and say what I feel:

_____

_____

_____

DAY 159   BEDTIME

Today has been the hundred-fifty-ninth day of my new smoke-free life. I look into my mirror and say what I feel:

_____

_____

_____

_____

_____   _____

Today's date   My signature

DAY 160   MORNING

Today I celebrate myself and my achievement. I look into my mirror and say what I feel:

_____

_____

_____

DAY 160   BEDTIME

Today has been the hundred-sixtieth day of my new smoke-free life. I look into my mirror and say what I feel:

_____

_____

_____

_____

_____   _____

Today's date   My signature

Continue to Build . . .
Your First Year
—Smoke-Free Log—

DAY 161   MORNING
Today I celebrate myself and my achievement. I look into my mirror and say what I feel:

_____

_____

_____

DAY 161   BEDTIME
Today has been the hundred-sixty-first day of my new smoke-free life. I look into my mirror and say what I feel:

_____

_____

_____

_____

_____   _____
Today's date   My signature

DAY 162   MORNING
Today I celebrate myself and my achievement. I look into my mirror and say what I feel:

_____

_____

_____

DAY 162   BEDTIME
Today has been the hundred-sixty-second day of my new smoke-free life. I look into my mirror and say what I feel:

_____

_____

_____

_____

_____   _____
Today's date   My signature

Continue to Build . . .
Your First Year
—Smoke-Free Log—

DAY 163   MORNING
Today I celebrate myself and my achievement. I look into my mirror and say what I feel:

_____

_____

_____

DAY 163   BEDTIME
Today has been the hundred-sixty-third day of my new smoke-free life. I look into my mirror and say what I feel:

_____

_____

_____

_____

_____   _____
Today's date   My signature

DAY 164   MORNING
Today I celebrate myself and my achievement. I look into my mirror and say what I feel:

_____

_____

_____

DAY 164   BEDTIME
Today has been the hundred-sixty-fourth day of my new smoke-free life. I look into my mirror and say what I feel:

_____

_____

_____

_____

_____   _____
Today's date   My signature

Continue to Build . . .
Your First Year
—Smoke-Free Log—

DAY 165   MORNING

Today I celebrate myself and my achievement. I look into my mirror and say what I feel:

_____

_____

_____

DAY 165   BEDTIME

Today has been the hundred-sixty-fifth day of my new smoke-free life. I look into my mirror and say what I feel:

_____

_____

_____

_____

_____   _____
Today's date   My signature

DAY 166   MORNING

Today I celebrate myself and my achievement. I look into my mirror and say what I feel:

_____

_____

_____

DAY 166   BEDTIME

Today has been the hundred-sixty-sixth day of my new smoke-free life. I look into my mirror and say what I feel:

_____

_____

_____

_____

_____   _____
Today's date   My signature

Continue to Build . . .
Your First Year
—Smoke-Free Log—

DAY 167   MORNING
Today I celebrate myself and my achievement. I look into my mirror
and say what I feel:

_____

_____

_____

DAY 167   BEDTIME
Today has been the hundred-sixty-seventh day of my new smoke-free
life. I look into my mirror and say what I feel:

_____

_____

_____

_____

_____   _____

Today's date   My signature

DAY 168   MORNING
Today I celebrate myself and my achievement. I look into my mirror
and say what I feel:

_____

_____

_____

DAY 168   BEDTIME
Today has been the hundred-sixty-eighth day of my new smoke-free
life. I look into my mirror and say what I feel:

_____

_____

_____

_____

_____   _____

Today's date   My signature

Continue to Build . . .
Your First Year
—Smoke-Free Log—

DAY 169   MORNING
Today I celebrate myself and my achievement. I look into my mirror and say what I feel:

_____

_____

_____

DAY 169   BEDTIME
Today has been the hundred-sixty-ninth day of my new smoke-free life. I look into my mirror and say what I feel:

_____

_____

_____

_____

_____   _____
Today's date   My signature

DAY 170   MORNING
Today I celebrate myself and my achievement. I look into my mirror and say what I feel:

_____

_____

_____

DAY 170   BEDTIME
Today has been the hundred-seventieth day of my new smoke-free life. I look into my mirror and say what I feel:

_____

_____

_____

_____

_____   _____
Today's date   My signature

Continue to Build . . .
Your First Year
—Smoke-Free Log—

DAY 171   MORNING
Today I celebrate myself and my achievement. I look into my mirror and say what I feel:

_____

_____

_____

DAY 171   BEDTIME
Today has been the hundred-seventy-first day of my new smoke-free life. I look into my mirror and say what I feel:

_____

_____

_____

_____

_____   _____
Today's date   My signature

DAY 172   MORNING
Today I celebrate myself and my achievement. I look into my mirror and say what I feel:

_____

_____

_____

DAY 172   BEDTIME
Today has been the hundred-seventy-second day of my new smoke-free life. I look into my mirror and say what I feel:

_____

_____

_____

_____

_____   _____
Today's date   My signature

Continue to Build . . .
Your First Year
—Smoke-Free Log—

DAY 173   MORNING

Today I celebrate myself and my achievement. I look into my mirror and say what I feel:

_____

_____

_____

DAY 173   BEDTIME

Today has been the hundred-seventy-third day of my new smoke-free life. I look into my mirror and say what I feel:

_____

_____

_____

_____

_____   _____

Today's date   My signature

DAY 174   MORNING

Today I celebrate myself and my achievement. I look into my mirror and say what I feel:

_____

_____

_____

DAY 174   BEDTIME

Today has been the hundred-seventy-fourth day of my new smoke-free life. I look into my mirror and say what I feel:

_____

_____

_____

_____

_____   _____

Today's date   My signature

Continue to Build . . .
Your First Year
—Smoke-Free Log—

DAY 175   MORNING

Today I celebrate myself and my achievement. I look into my mirror
and say what I feel:

_____

_____

_____

DAY 175   BEDTIME

Today has been the hundred-seventy-fifth day of my new smoke-free
life. I look into my mirror and say what I feel:

_____

_____

_____

_____

_____   _____

Today's date   My signature

DAY 176   MORNING

Today I celebrate myself and my achievement. I look into my mirror
and say what I feel:

_____

_____

_____

DAY 176   BEDTIME

Today has been the hundred-seventy-sixth day of my new smoke-free
life. I look into my mirror and say what I feel:

_____

_____

_____

_____

_____   _____

Today's date   My signature

Continue to Build . . .
Your First Year
—Smoke-Free Log—

DAY 177   MORNING

Today I celebrate myself and my achievement. I look into my mirror and say what I feel:

_____

_____

_____

DAY 177   BEDTIME

Today has been the hundred-seventy-seventh day of my new smoke-free life. I look into my mirror and say what I feel:

_____

_____

_____

_____

_____   _____

Today's date   My signature

DAY 178   MORNING

Today I celebrate myself and my achievement. I look into my mirror and say what I feel:

_____

_____

_____

DAY 178   BEDTIME

Today has been the hundred-seventy-eighth day of my new smoke-free life. I look into my mirror and say what I feel:

_____

_____

_____

_____

_____   _____

Today's date   My signature

Continue to Build . . .
Your First Year
—Smoke-Free Log—

DAY 179   MORNING
Today I celebrate myself and my achievement. I look into my mirror and say what I feel:

_____

_____

_____

DAY 179   BEDTIME
Today has been the hundred-seventy-ninth day of my new smoke-free life. I look into my mirror and say what I feel:

_____

_____

_____

_____

_____   _____

Today's date   My signature

DAY 180   MORNING
Today I celebrate myself and my achievement. I look into my mirror and say what I feel:

_____

_____

_____

DAY 180   BEDTIME
Today has been the hundred-eightieth day of my new smoke-free life. I look into my mirror and say what I feel:

_____

_____

_____

_____

_____   _____

Today's date   My signature

Continue to Build . . .
Your First Year
—Smoke-Free Log—

DAY 181   MORNING

Today I celebrate myself and my achievement. I look into my mirror and say what I feel:

_____

_____

_____

DAY 181   BEDTIME

Today has been the hundred-eighty-first day of my new smoke-free life. I look into my mirror and say what I feel:

_____

_____

_____

_____

_____   _____
Today's date   My signature

DAY 182   MORNING

Today I celebrate myself and my achievement. I look into my mirror and say what I feel:

_____

_____

_____

DAY 182   BEDTIME

Today has been the hundred-eighty-second day of my new smoke-free life. I look into my mirror and say what I feel:

_____

_____

_____

_____

_____   _____
Today's date   My signature

Continue to Build . . .
Your First Year
—Smoke-Free Log—

DAY 183   MORNING

Today I celebrate myself and my achievement. I look into my mirror and say what I feel:

_____

_____

_____

DAY 183   BEDTIME

Today has been the hundred-eighty-third day of my new smoke-free life. I look into my mirror and say what I feel:

_____

_____

_____

_____

_____   _____

Today's date   My signature

DAY 184   MORNING

Today I celebrate myself and my achievement. I look into my mirror and say what I feel:

_____

_____

_____

DAY 184   BEDTIME

Today has been the hundred-eighty-fourth day of my new smoke-free life. I look into my mirror and say what I feel:

_____

_____

_____

_____

_____   _____

Today's date   My signature

Continue to Build . . .
Your First Year
—Smoke-Free Log—

DAY 185   MORNING

Today I celebrate myself and my achievement. I look into my mirror and say what I feel:

_____

_____

_____

DAY 185   BEDTIME

Today has been the hundred-eighty-fifth day of my new smoke-free life. I look into my mirror and say what I feel:

_____

_____

_____

_____

_____   _____
Today's date   My signature

DAY 186   MORNING

Today I celebrate myself and my achievement. I look into my mirror and say what I feel:

_____

_____

_____

DAY 186   BEDTIME

Today has been the hundred-eighty-sixth day of my new smoke-free life. I look into my mirror and say what I feel:

_____

_____

_____

_____

_____   _____
Today's date   My signature

Continue to Build . . .
Your First Year
—Smoke-Free Log—

DAY 187   MORNING
Today I celebrate myself and my achievement. I look into my mirror and say what I feel:

_____

_____

_____

DAY 187   BEDTIME
Today has been the hundred-eighty-seventh day of my new smoke-free life. I look into my mirror and say what I feel:

_____

_____

_____

_____

_____   _____

Today's date   My signature

DAY 188   MORNING
Today I celebrate myself and my achievement. I look into my mirror and say what I feel:

_____

_____

_____

DAY 188   BEDTIME
Today has been the hundred-eighty-eighth day of my new smoke-free life. I look into my mirror and say what I feel:

_____

_____

_____

_____

_____   _____

Today's date   My signature

Continue to Build . . .
Your First Year
—Smoke-Free Log—

DAY 189   MORNING
Today I celebrate myself and my achievement. I look into my mirror and say what I feel:

_____

_____

_____

DAY 189   BEDTIME
Today has been the hundred-eighty-ninth day of my new smoke-free life. I look into my mirror and say what I feel:

_____

_____

_____

_____

_____   _____

Today's date   My signature

DAY 190   MORNING
Today I celebrate myself and my achievement. I look into my mirror and say what I feel:

_____

_____

_____

DAY 190   BEDTIME
Today has been the hundred-ninetieth day of my new smoke-free life. I look into my mirror and say what I feel:

_____

_____

_____

_____

_____   _____

Today's date   My signature

Continue to Build . . .
Your First Year
—Smoke-Free Log—

DAY 191   MORNING
Today I celebrate myself and my achievement. I look into my mirror and say what I feel:

_____

_____

_____

DAY 191   BEDTIME
Today has been the hundred-ninety-first day of my new smoke-free life. I look into my mirror and say what I feel:

_____

_____

_____

_____

_____   _____
Today's date   My signature

DAY 192   MORNING
Today I celebrate myself and my achievement. I look into my mirror and say what I feel:

_____

_____

_____

DAY 192   BEDTIME
Today has been the hundred-ninety-second day of my new smoke-free life. I look into my mirror and say what I feel:

_____

_____

_____

_____

_____   _____
Today's date   My signature

Continue to Build . . .
Your First Year
—Smoke-Free Log—

DAY 193   MORNING
Today I celebrate myself and my achievement. I look into my mirror and say what I feel:

_____

_____

_____

DAY 193   BEDTIME
Today has been the hundred-ninety-third day of my new smoke-free life. I look into my mirror and say what I feel:

_____

_____

_____

_____

_____   _____
Today's date   My signature

DAY 194   MORNING
Today I celebrate myself and my achievement. I look into my mirror and say what I feel:

_____

_____

_____

DAY 194   BEDTIME
Today has been the hundred-ninety-fourth day of my new smoke-free life. I look into my mirror and say what I feel:

_____

_____

_____

_____

_____   _____
Today's date   My signature

Continue to Build . . .
Your First Year
—Smoke-Free Log—

DAY 195   MORNING

Today I celebrate myself and my achievement. I look into my mirror and say what I feel:

_____

_____

_____

DAY 195   BEDTIME

Today has been the hundred-ninety-fifth day of my new smoke-free life. I look into my mirror and say what I feel:

_____

_____

_____

_____

_____   _____

Today's date   My signature

DAY 196   MORNING

Today I celebrate myself and my achievement. I look into my mirror and say what I feel:

_____

_____

_____

DAY 196   BEDTIME

Today has been the hundred-ninety-sixth day of my new smoke-free life. I look into my mirror and say what I feel:

_____

_____

_____

_____

_____   _____

Today's date   My signature

Continue to Build . . .
Your First Year
—Smoke-Free Log—

DAY 197   MORNING
Today I celebrate myself and my achievement. I look into my mirror and say what I feel:

_____
_____
_____

DAY 197   BEDTIME
Today has been the hundred-ninety-seventh day of my new smoke-free life. I look into my mirror and say what I feel:

_____
_____
_____
_____

_____   _____
Today's date   My signature

DAY 198   MORNING
Today I celebrate myself and my achievement. I look into my mirror and say what I feel:

_____
_____
_____

DAY 198   BEDTIME
Today has been the hundred-ninety-eighth day of my new smoke-free life. I look into my mirror and say what I feel:

_____
_____
_____
_____

_____   _____
Today's date   My signature

Continue to Build . . .
Your First Year
—Smoke-Free Log—

DAY 199   MORNING
Today I celebrate myself and my achievement. I look into my mirror and say what I feel:

_____

_____

_____

DAY 199   BEDTIME
Today has been the hundred-ninety-ninth day of my new smoke-free life. I look into my mirror and say what I feel:

_____

_____

_____

_____

_____   _____

Today's date   My signature

DAY 200   MORNING
Today I celebrate myself and my achievement. I look into my mirror and say what I feel:

_____

_____

_____

DAY 200   BEDTIME
Today has been the two-hundredth day of my new smoke-free life. I look into my mirror and say what I feel:

_____

_____

_____

_____

_____   _____

Today's date   My signature

Continue to Build . . .
Your First Year
—Smoke-Free Log—

DAY 201   **MORNING**

Today I celebrate myself and my achievement. I look into my mirror and say what I feel:

_____
_____
_____

DAY 201   **BEDTIME**

Today has been the two-hundred-first day of my new smoke-free life. I look into my mirror and say what I feel:

_____
_____
_____
_____

_____   _____
Today's date   My signature

DAY 202   **MORNING**

Today I celebrate myself and my achievement. I look into my mirror and say what I feel:

_____
_____
_____

DAY 202   **BEDTIME**

Today has been the two-hundred-second day of my new smoke-free life. I look into my mirror and say what I feel:

_____
_____
_____
_____

_____   _____
Today's date   My signature

Continue to Build . . .
Your First Year
—Smoke-Free Log—

DAY 203   MORNING
Today I celebrate myself and my achievement. I look into my mirror and say what I feel:

_____

_____

_____

DAY 203   BEDTIME
Today has been the two-hundred-third day of my new smoke-free life. I look into my mirror and say what I feel:

_____

_____

_____

_____

_____   _____

Today's date   My signature

DAY 204   MORNING
Today I celebrate myself and my achievement. I look into my mirror and say what I feel:

_____

_____

_____

DAY 204   BEDTIME
Today has been the two-hundred-fourth day of my new smoke-free life. I look into my mirror and say what I feel:

_____

_____

_____

_____

_____   _____

Today's date   My signature

Continue to Build...
Your First Year
—Smoke-Free Log—

DAY 205   MORNING
Today I celebrate myself and my achievement. I look into my mirror and say what I feel:

_____
_____
_____

DAY 205   BEDTIME
Today has been the two-hundred-fifth day of my new smoke-free life. I look into my mirror and say what I feel:

_____
_____
_____
_____

_____   _____
Today's date   My signature

DAY 206   MORNING
Today I celebrate myself and my achievement. I look into my mirror and say what I feel:

_____
_____
_____

DAY 206   BEDTIME
Today has been the two-hundred-sixth day of my new smoke-free life. I look into my mirror and say what I feel:

_____
_____
_____
_____

_____   _____
Today's date   My signature

Continue to Build . . .
Your First Year
—Smoke-Free Log—

DAY 207   MORNING
Today I celebrate myself and my achievement. I look into my mirror and say what I feel:

_____

_____

_____

DAY 207   BEDTIME
Today has been the two-hundred-seventh day of my new smoke-free life. I look into my mirror and say what I feel:

_____

_____

_____

_____

_____   _____
Today's date   My signature

DAY 208   MORNING
Today I celebrate myself and my achievement. I look into my mirror and say what I feel:

_____

_____

_____

DAY 208   BEDTIME
Today has been the two-hundred-eighth day of my new smoke-free life. I look into my mirror and say what I feel:

_____

_____

_____

_____   _____
Today's date   My signature

Continue to Build . . .
Your First Year
—Smoke-Free Log—

DAY 209 MORNING
Today I celebrate myself and my achievement. I look into my mirror and say what I feel:

_____

_____

_____

DAY 209 BEDTIME
Today has been the two-hundred-ninth day of my new smoke-free life. I look into my mirror and say what I feel:

_____

_____

_____

_____

_____   _____
Today's date   My signature

DAY 210 MORNING
Today I celebrate myself and my achievement. I look into my mirror and say what I feel:

_____

_____

_____

DAY 210 BEDTIME
Today has been the two-hundred-tenth day of my new smoke-free life. I look into my mirror and say what I feel:

_____

_____

_____

_____

_____   _____
Today's date   My signature

Continue to Build . . .
Your First Year
—Smoke-Free Log—

DAY 211   MORNING

Today I celebrate myself and my achievement. I look into my mirror and say what I feel:

_____

_____

_____

DAY 211   BEDTIME

Today has been the two-hundred-eleventh day of my new smoke-free life. I look into my mirror and say what I feel:

_____

_____

_____

_____

_____   _____

Today's date   My signature

DAY 212   MORNING

Today I celebrate myself and my achievement. I look into my mirror and say what I feel:

_____

_____

_____

DAY 212   BEDTIME

Today has been the two-hundred-twelfth day of my new smoke-free life. I look into my mirror and say what I feel:

_____

_____

_____

_____

_____   _____

Today's date   My signature

Continue to Build . . .
Your First Year
—Smoke-Free Log—

DAY 213   MORNING

Today I celebrate myself and my achievement. I look into my mirror and say what I feel:

_____

_____

_____

DAY 213   BEDTIME

Today has been the two-hundred-thirteenth day of my new smoke-free life. I look into my mirror and say what I feel:

_____

_____

_____

_____

_____   _____

Today's date   My signature

DAY 214   MORNING

Today I celebrate myself and my achievement. I look into my mirror and say what I feel:

_____

_____

_____

DAY 214   BEDTIME

Today has been the two-hundred-fourteenth day of my new smoke-free life. I look into my mirror and say what I feel:

_____

_____

_____

_____

_____   _____

Today's date   My signature

Continue to Build . . .
Your First Year
—Smoke-Free Log—

DAY 215   MORNING

Today I celebrate myself and my achievement. I look into my mirror and say what I feel:

_____

_____

_____

DAY 215   BEDTIME

Today has been the two-hundred-fifteenth day of my new smoke-free life. I look into my mirror and say what I feel:

_____

_____

_____

_____

_____   _____

Today's date   My signature

DAY 216   MORNING

Today I celebrate myself and my achievement. I look into my mirror and say what I feel:

_____

_____

_____

DAY 216   BEDTIME

Today has been the two-hundred-sixteenth day of my new smoke-free life. I look into my mirror and say what I feel:

_____

_____

_____

_____

_____   _____

Today's date   My signature

Continue to Build . . .
Your First Year
—Smoke-Free Log—

DAY 217   MORNING

Today I celebrate myself and my achievement. I look into my mirror and say what I feel:

_____

_____

_____

DAY 217   BEDTIME

Today has been the two-hundred-seventeenth day of my new smoke-free life. I look into my mirror and say what I feel:

_____

_____

_____

_____

_____   _____

Today's date   My signature

DAY 218   MORNING

Today I celebrate myself and my achievement. I look into my mirror and say what I feel:

_____

_____

_____

DAY 218   BEDTIME

Today has been the two-hundred-eighteenth day of my new smoke-free life. I look into my mirror and say what I feel:

_____

_____

_____

_____

_____   _____

Today's date   My signature

Continue to Build . . .
Your First Year
—Smoke-Free Log—

DAY 219   MORNING
Today I celebrate myself and my achievement. I look into my mirror and say what I feel:

_____
_____

DAY 219   BEDTIME
Today has been the two-hundred-nineteenth day of my new smoke-free life. I look into my mirror and say what I feel:

_____
_____
_____
_____

_____   _____
Today's date   My signature

DAY 220   MORNING
Today I celebrate myself and my achievement. I look into my mirror and say what I feel:

_____
_____

DAY 220   BEDTIME
Today has been the two-hundred-twentieth day of my new smoke-free life. I look into my mirror and say what I feel:

_____
_____
_____
_____

_____   _____
Today's date   My signature

Continue to Build . . .
Your First Year
—Smoke-Free Log—

DAY 221   MORNING

Today I celebrate myself and my achievement. I look into my mirror and say what I feel:

_____

_____

_____

DAY 221   BEDTIME

Today has been the two-hundred-twenty-first day of my new smoke-free life. I look into my mirror and say what I feel:

_____

_____

_____

_____

_____   _____
Today's date   My signature

DAY 222   MORNING

Today I celebrate myself and my achievement. I look into my mirror and say what I feel:

_____

_____

_____

DAY 222   BEDTIME

Today has been the two-hundred-twenty-second day of my new smoke-free life. I look into my mirror and say what I feel:

_____

_____

_____

_____

_____   _____
Today's date   My signature

Continue to Build . . .
Your First Year
—Smoke-Free Log—

DAY 223   MORNING

Today I celebrate myself and my achievement. I look into my mirror and say what I feel:

_____

_____

_____

DAY 223   BEDTIME

Today has been the two-hundred-twenty-third day of my new smoke-free life. I look into my mirror and say what I feel:

_____

_____

_____

_____

_____   _____

Today's date   My signature

DAY 224   MORNING

Today I celebrate myself and my achievement. I look into my mirror and say what I feel:

_____

_____

_____

DAY 224   BEDTIME

Today has been the two-hundred-twenty-fourth day of my new smoke-free life. I look into my mirror and say what I feel:

_____

_____

_____

_____

_____   _____

Today's date   My signature

Continue to Build . . .
Your First Year
—Smoke-Free Log—

DAY 225   MORNING
Today I celebrate myself and my achievement. I look into my mirror and say what I feel:

_____

_____

_____

DAY 225   BEDTIME
Today has been the two-hundred-twenty-fifth day of my new smoke-free life. I look into my mirror and say what I feel:

_____

_____

_____

_____

_____   _____
Today's date   My signature

DAY 226   MORNING
Today I celebrate myself and my achievement. I look into my mirror and say what I feel:

_____

_____

_____

DAY 226   BEDTIME
Today has been the two-hundred-twenty-sixth day of my new smoke-free life. I look into my mirror and say what I feel:

_____

_____

_____

_____   _____
Today's date   My signature

Continue to Build . . .
Your First Year
—Smoke-Free Log—

DAY 227   MORNING
Today I celebrate myself and my achievement. I look into my mirror and say what I feel:

_____

_____

_____

DAY 227   BEDTIME
Today has been the two-hundred-twenty-seventh day of my new smoke-free life. I look into my mirror and say what I feel:

_____

_____

_____

_____

_____   _____
Today's date   My signature

DAY 228   MORNING
Today I celebrate myself and my achievement. I look into my mirror and say what I feel:

_____

_____

_____

DAY 228   BEDTIME
Today has been the two-hundred-twenty-eighth day of my new smoke-free life. I look into my mirror and say what I feel:

_____

_____

_____

_____

_____   _____
Today's date   My signature

Continue to Build . . .
Your First Year
—Smoke-Free Log—

DAY 229   MORNING

Today I celebrate myself and my achievement. I look into my mirror and say what I feel:

_____

_____

DAY 229   BEDTIME

Today has been the two-hundred-twenty-ninth day of my new smoke-free life. I look into my mirror and say what I feel:

_____

_____

_____

_____

_____   _____
Today's date   My signature

DAY 230   MORNING

Today I celebrate myself and my achievement. I look into my mirror and say what I feel:

_____

_____

DAY 230   BEDTIME

Today has been the two-hundred-thirtieth day of my new smoke-free life. I look into my mirror and say what I feel:

_____

_____

_____

_____

_____   _____
Today's date   My signature

Continue to Build . . .
Your First Year
—Smoke-Free Log—

DAY 231   MORNING
Today I celebrate myself and my achievement. I look into my mirror and say what I feel:

_____

_____

_____

DAY 231   BEDTIME
Today has been the two-hundred-thirty-first day of my new smoke-free life. I look into my mirror and say what I feel:

_____

_____

_____

_____

_____   _____
Today's date   My signature

DAY 232   MORNING
Today I celebrate myself and my achievement. I look into my mirror and say what I feel:

_____

_____

_____

DAY 232   BEDTIME
Today has been the two-hundred-thirty-second day of my new smoke-free life. I look into my mirror and say what I feel:

_____

_____

_____

_____

_____   _____
Today's date   My signature

Continue to Build . . .
Your First Year
—Smoke-Free Log—

DAY 233   MORNING
Today I celebrate myself and my achievement. I look into my mirror and say what I feel:

_____

_____

DAY 233   BEDTIME
Today has been the two-hundred-thirty-third day of my new smoke-free life. I look into my mirror and say what I feel:

_____

_____

_____

_____   _____
Today's date   My signature

DAY 234   MORNING
Today I celebrate myself and my achievement. I look into my mirror and say what I feel:

_____

_____

DAY 234   BEDTIME
Today has been the two-hundred-thirty-fourth day of my new smoke-free life. I look into my mirror and say what I feel:

_____

_____

_____

_____   _____
Today's date   My signature

Continue to Build . . .
Your First Year
—Smoke-Free Log—

DAY 235   MORNING

Today I celebrate myself and my achievement. I look into my mirror and say what I feel:

_____

_____

_____

DAY 235   BEDTIME

Today has been the two-hundred-thirty-fifth day of my new smoke-free life. I look into my mirror and say what I feel:

_____

_____

_____

_____

_____   _____
Today's date   My signature

DAY 236   MORNING

Today I celebrate myself and my achievement. I look into my mirror and say what I feel:

_____

_____

_____

DAY 236   BEDTIME

Today has been the two-hundred-thirty-sixth day of my new smoke-free life. I look into my mirror and say what I feel:

_____

_____

_____

_____

_____   _____
Today's date   My signature

Continue to Build . . .
Your First Year
—Smoke-Free Log—

DAY 237   MORNING

Today I celebrate myself and my achievement. I look into my mirror and say what I feel:

_____

_____

_____

DAY 237   BEDTIME

Today has been the two-hundred-thirty-seventh day of my new smoke-free life. I look into my mirror and say what I feel:

_____

_____

_____

_____

_____   _____

Today's date   My signature

DAY 238   MORNING

Today I celebrate myself and my achievement. I look into my mirror and say what I feel:

_____

_____

_____

DAY 238   BEDTIME

Today has been the two-hundred-thirty-eighth day of my new smoke-free life. I look into my mirror and say what I feel:

_____

_____

_____

_____

_____   _____

Today's date   My signature

Continue to Build . . .
Your First Year
—Smoke-Free Log—

DAY 239   MORNING
Today I celebrate myself and my achievement. I look into my mirror and say what I feel:

_____

_____

_____

DAY 239   BEDTIME
Today has been the two-hundred-thirty-ninth day of my new smoke-free life. I look into my mirror and say what I feel:

_____

_____

_____

_____

Today's date   My signature

DAY 240   MORNING
Today I celebrate myself and my achievement. I look into my mirror and say what I feel:

_____

_____

_____

DAY 240   BEDTIME
Today has been the two-hundred-fortieth day of my new smoke-free life. I look into my mirror and say what I feel:

_____

_____

_____

_____

Today's date   My signature

Continue to Build . . .
Your First Year
—Smoke-Free Log—

DAY 241   MORNING
Today I celebrate myself and my achievement. I look into my mirror and say what I feel:

_____

_____

_____

DAY 241   BEDTIME
Today has been the two-hundred-forty-first day of my new smoke-free life. I look into my mirror and say what I feel:

_____

_____

_____

_____

_____   _____
Today's date   My signature

DAY 242   MORNING
Today I celebrate myself and my achievement. I look into my mirror and say what I feel:

_____

_____

_____

DAY 242   BEDTIME
Today has been the two-hundred-forty-second day of my new smoke-free life. I look into my mirror and say what I feel:

_____

_____

_____

_____   _____
Today's date   My signature

Continue to Build . . .
Your First Year
—Smoke-Free Log—

DAY 243   MORNING

Today I celebrate myself and my achievement. I look into my mirror and say what I feel:

_____

_____

_____

DAY 243   BEDTIME

Today has been the two-hundred-forty-third day of my new smoke-free life. I look into my mirror and say what I feel:

_____

_____

_____

_____

_____   _____

Today's date   My signature

DAY 244   MORNING

Today I celebrate myself and my achievement. I look into my mirror and say what I feel:

_____

_____

_____

DAY 244   BEDTIME

Today has been the two-hundred-forty-fourth day of my new smoke-free life. I look into my mirror and say what I feel:

_____

_____

_____

_____

_____   _____

Today's date   My signature

Continue to Build . . .
Your First Year
—Smoke-Free Log—

DAY 245   MORNING

Today I celebrate myself and my achievement. I look into my mirror and say what I feel:

_____

_____

_____

DAY 245   BEDTIME

Today has been the two-hundred-forty-fifth day of my new smoke-free life. I look into my mirror and say what I feel:

_____

_____

_____

_____

_____   _____

Today's date   My signature

DAY 246   MORNING

Today I celebrate myself and my achievement. I look into my mirror and say what I feel:

_____

_____

_____

DAY 246   BEDTIME

Today has been the two-hundred-forty-sixth day of my new smoke-free life. I look into my mirror and say what I feel:

_____

_____

_____

_____

_____   _____

Today's date   My signature

Continue to Build . . .
Your First Year
—Smoke-Free Log—

DAY 247   MORNING

Today I celebrate myself and my achievement. I look into my mirror and say what I feel:

_____

_____

_____

DAY 247   BEDTIME

Today has been the two-hundred-forty-seventh day of my new smoke-free life. I look into my mirror and say what I feel:

_____

_____

_____

_____

_____

Today's date   My signature

DAY 248   MORNING

Today I celebrate myself and my achievement. I look into my mirror and say what I feel:

_____

_____

_____

DAY 248   BEDTIME

Today has been the two-hundred-forty-eighth day of my new smoke-free life. I look into my mirror and say what I feel:

_____

_____

_____

_____

Today's date   My signature

Continue to Build...
Your First Year
—Smoke-Free Log—

DAY 249   MORNING

Today I celebrate myself and my achievement. I look into my mirror and say what I feel:

_____

_____

_____

DAY 249   BEDTIME

Today has been the two-hundred-forty-ninth day of my new smoke-free life. I look into my mirror and say what I feel:

_____

_____

_____

_____

_____   _____

Today's date   My signature

DAY 250   MORNING

Today I celebrate myself and my achievement. I look into my mirror and say what I feel:

_____

_____

_____

DAY 250   BEDTIME

Today has been the two-hundred-fiftieth day of my new smoke-free life. I look into my mirror and say what I feel:

_____

_____

_____

_____

_____   _____

Today's date   My signature

Continue to Build . . .
Your First Year
—Smoke-Free Log—

DAY 251   MORNING

Today I celebrate myself and my achievement. I look into my mirror and say what I feel:

_____

_____

DAY 251   BEDTIME

Today has been the two-hundred-fifty-first day of my new smoke-free life. I look into my mirror and say what I feel:

_____

_____

_____

_____

_____   _____
Today's date   My signature

DAY 252   MORNING

Today I celebrate myself and my achievement. I look into my mirror and say what I feel:

_____

_____

DAY 252   BEDTIME

Today has been the two-hundred-fifty-second day of my new smoke-free life. I look into my mirror and say what I feel:

_____

_____

_____

_____   _____
Today's date   My signature

Continue to Build . . .
Your First Year
—Smoke-Free Log—

DAY 253   MORNING
Today I celebrate myself and my achievement. I look into my mirror and say what I feel:

_____

_____
_____

DAY 253   BEDTIME
Today has been the two-hundred-fifty-third day of my new smoke-free life. I look into my mirror and say what I feel:

_____

_____
_____

_____

_____   _____
Today's date   My signature

DAY 254   MORNING
Today I celebrate myself and my achievement. I look into my mirror and say what I feel:

_____

_____
_____

DAY 254   BEDTIME
Today has been the two-hundred-fifty-fourth day of my new smoke-free life. I look into my mirror and say what I feel:

_____

_____
_____

_____

_____   _____
Today's date   My signature

Continue to Build . . .
Your First Year
—Smoke-Free Log—

DAY 255   MORNING
Today I celebrate myself and my achievement. I look into my mirror and say what I feel:

_____

_____

_____

DAY 255   BEDTIME
Today has been the two-hundred-fifty-fifth day of my new smoke-free life. I look into my mirror and say what I feel:

_____

_____

_____

_____

_____   _____
Today's date   My signature

DAY 256   MORNING
Today I celebrate myself and my achievement. I look into my mirror and say what I feel:

_____

_____

_____

DAY 256   BEDTIME
Today has been the two-hundred-fifty-sixth day of my new smoke-free life. I look into my mirror and say what I feel:

_____

_____

_____

_____

_____   _____
Today's date   My signature

Continue to Build . . .
Your First Year
—Smoke-Free Log—

DAY 257   MORNING

Today I celebrate myself and my achievement. I look into my mirror and say what I feel:

_____

_____

_____

DAY 257   BEDTIME

Today has been the two-hundred-fifty-seventh day of my new smoke-free life. I look into my mirror and say what I feel:

_____

_____

_____

_____

_____   _____
Today's date   My signature

DAY 258   MORNING

Today I celebrate myself and my achievement. I look into my mirror and say what I feel:

_____

_____

_____

DAY 258   BEDTIME

Today has been the two-hundred-fifty-eighth day of my new smoke-free life. I look into my mirror and say what I feel:

_____

_____

_____

_____

_____   _____
Today's date   My signature

Continue to Build . . .
Your First Year
—Smoke-Free Log—

DAY 259   MORNING
Today I celebrate myself and my achievement. I look into my mirror and say what I feel:

_____

_____

_____

DAY 259   BEDTIME
Today has been the two-hundred-fifty-ninth day of my new smoke-free life. I look into my mirror and say what I feel:

_____

_____

_____

_____

_____   _____
Today's date   My signature

DAY 260   MORNING
Today I celebrate myself and my achievement. I look into my mirror and say what I feel:

_____

_____

_____

DAY 260   BEDTIME
Today has been the two-hundred-sixtieth day of my new smoke-free life. I look into my mirror and say what I feel:

_____

_____

_____

_____

_____   _____
Today's date   My signature

Continue to Build . . .
Your First Year
—Smoke-Free Log—

DAY 261   MORNING
Today I celebrate myself and my achievement. I look into my mirror and say what I feel:

_____

_____

_____

DAY 261   BEDTIME
Today has been the two-hundred-sixty-first day of my new smoke-free life. I look into my mirror and say what I feel:

_____

_____

_____

_____

_____   _____
Today's date   My signature

DAY 262   MORNING
Today I celebrate myself and my achievement. I look into my mirror and say what I feel:

_____

_____

_____

DAY 262   BEDTIME
Today has been the two-hundred-sixty-second day of my new smoke-free life. I look into my mirror and say what I feel:

_____

_____

_____

_____

_____   _____
Today's date   My signature

Continue to Build . . .
Your First Year
—Smoke-Free Log—

DAY 263   MORNING
Today I celebrate myself and my achievement. I look into my mirror
and say what I feel:

_____

_____

_____

DAY 263   BEDTIME
Today has been the two-hundred-sixty-third day of my new smoke-
free life. I look into my mirror and say what I feel:

_____

_____

_____

_____

_____   _____
Today's date   My signature

DAY 264   MORNING
Today I celebrate myself and my achievement. I look into my mirror
and say what I feel:

_____

_____

_____

DAY 264   BEDTIME
Today has been the two-hundred-sixty-fourth day of my new smoke-
free life. I look into my mirror and say what I feel:

_____

_____

_____

_____

_____   _____
Today's date   My signature

Continue to Build . . .
Your First Year
—Smoke-Free Log—

DAY 265   MORNING
Today I celebrate myself and my achievement. I look into my mirror and say what I feel:

_____

_____

DAY 265   BEDTIME
Today has been the two-hundred-sixty-fifth day of my new smoke-free life. I look into my mirror and say what I feel:

_____

_____

_____

_____

_____   _____
Today's date   My signature

DAY 266   MORNING
Today I celebrate myself and my achievement. I look into my mirror and say what I feel:

_____

_____

DAY 266   BEDTIME
Today has been the two-hundred-sixty-sixth day of my new smoke-free life. I look into my mirror and say what I feel:

_____

_____

_____

_____   _____
Today's date   My signature

Continue to Build . . .
Your First Year
—Smoke-Free Log—

DAY 267   MORNING

Today I celebrate myself and my achievement. I look into my mirror and say what I feel:

_____

_____

_____

DAY 267   BEDTIME

Today has been the two-hundred-sixty-seventh day of my new smoke-free life. I look into my mirror and say what I feel:

_____

_____

_____

_____

_____   _____

Today's date   My signature

DAY 268   MORNING

Today I celebrate myself and my achievement. I look into my mirror and say what I feel:

_____

_____

_____

DAY 268   BEDTIME

Today has been the two-hundred-sixty-eighth day of my new smoke-free life. I look into my mirror and say what I feel:

_____

_____

_____

_____

_____   _____

Today's date   My signature

Continue to Build . . .
Your First Year
—Smoke-Free Log—

DAY 269   MORNING

Today I celebrate myself and my achievement. I look into my mirror and say what I feel:

_____

_____

_____

DAY 269   BEDTIME

Today has been the two-hundred-sixty-ninth day of my new smoke-free life. I look into my mirror and say what I feel:

_____

_____

_____

_____

_____   _____
Today's date   My signature

DAY 270   MORNING

Today I celebrate myself and my achievement. I look into my mirror and say what I feel:

_____

_____

_____

DAY 270   BEDTIME

Today has been the two-hundred-seventieth day of my new smoke-free life. I look into my mirror and say what I feel:

_____

_____

_____

_____

_____   _____
Today's date   My signature

Continue to Build . . .
Your First Year
—Smoke-Free Log—

DAY 271   MORNING
Today I celebrate myself and my achievement. I look into my mirror and say what I feel:

_____

_____

_____

DAY 271   BEDTIME
Today has been the two-hundred-seventy-first day of my new smoke-free life. I look into my mirror and say what I feel:

_____

_____

_____

_____

_____   _____
Today's date   My signature

DAY 272   MORNING
Today I celebrate myself and my achievement. I look into my mirror and say what I feel:

_____

_____

_____

DAY 272   BEDTIME
Today has been the two-hundred-seventy-second day of my new smoke-free life. I look into my mirror and say what I feel:

_____

_____

_____

_____

_____   _____
Today's date   My signature

Continue to Build . . .
Your First Year
—Smoke-Free Log—

DAY 273   MORNING

Today I celebrate myself and my achievement. I look into my mirror and say what I feel:

_____

_____

_____

DAY 273   BEDTIME

Today has been the two-hundred-seventy-third day of my new smoke-free life. I look into my mirror and say what I feel:

_____

_____

_____

_____

_____   _____

Today's date   My signature

DAY 274   MORNING

Today I celebrate myself and my achievement. I look into my mirror and say what I feel:

_____

_____

_____

DAY 274   BEDTIME

Today has been the two-hundred-seventy-fourth day of my new smoke-free life. I look into my mirror and say what I feel:

_____

_____

_____

_____

_____   _____

Today's date   My signature

Continue to Build . . .
Your First Year
—Smoke-Free Log—

DAY 275   MORNING

Today I celebrate myself and my achievement. I look into my mirror and say what I feel:

_____

_____

DAY 275   BEDTIME

Today has been the two-hundred-seventy-fifth day of my new smoke-free life. I look into my mirror and say what I feel:

_____

_____

_____

_____

_____   _____
Today's date   My signature

DAY 276   MORNING

Today I celebrate myself and my achievement. I look into my mirror and say what I feel:

_____

_____

DAY 276   BEDTIME

Today has been the two-hundred-seventy-sixth day of my new smoke-free life. I look into my mirror and say what I feel:

_____

_____

_____

_____   _____
Today's date   My signature

Continue to Build . . .
Your First Year
—Smoke-Free Log—

DAY 277   MORNING
Today I celebrate myself and my achievement. I look into my mirror and say what I feel:

_____

_____

_____

DAY 277   BEDTIME
Today has been the two-hundred-seventy-seventh day of my new smoke-free life. I look into my mirror and say what I feel:

_____

_____

_____

_____

_____   _____
Today's date   My signature

DAY 278   MORNING
Today I celebrate myself and my achievement. I look into my mirror and say what I feel:

_____

_____

_____

DAY 278   BEDTIME
Today has been the two-hundred-seventy-eighth day of my new smoke-free life. I look into my mirror and say what I feel:

_____

_____

_____

_____   _____
Today's date   My signature

Continue to Build . . .
Your First Year
—Smoke-Free Log—

DAY 279   MORNING

Today I celebrate myself and my achievement. I look into my mirror and say what I feel:

_____

_____

_____

DAY 279   BEDTIME

Today has been the two-hundred-seventy-ninth day of my new smoke-free life. I look into my mirror and say what I feel:

_____

_____

_____

_____

_____   _____

Today's date   My signature

DAY 280   MORNING

Today I celebrate myself and my achievement. I look into my mirror and say what I feel:

_____

_____

_____

DAY 280   BEDTIME

Today has been the two-hundred-eightieth day of my new smoke-free life. I look into my mirror and say what I feel:

_____

_____

_____

_____

_____   _____

Today's date   My signature

Continue to Build . . .
Your First Year
—Smoke-Free Log—

DAY 281 MORNING
Today I celebrate myself and my achievement. I look into my mirror and say what I feel:

_____

_____

_____

DAY 281 BEDTIME
Today has been the two-hundred-eighty-first day of my new smoke-free life. I look into my mirror and say what I feel:

_____

_____

_____

_____

_____

Today's date   My signature

DAY 282 MORNING
Today I celebrate myself and my achievement. I look into my mirror and say what I feel:

_____

_____

_____

DAY 282 BEDTIME
Today has been the two-hundred-eighty-second day of my new smoke-free life. I look into my mirror and say what I feel:

_____

_____

_____

_____

_____

Today's date   My signature

Continue to Build . . .
Your First Year
—Smoke-Free Log—

DAY 283   MORNING

Today I celebrate myself and my achievement. I look into my mirror and say what I feel:

_____

_____

_____

DAY 283   BEDTIME

Today has been the two-hundred-eighty-third day of my new smoke-free life. I look into my mirror and say what I feel:

_____

_____

_____

_____

_____   _____

Today's date   My signature

DAY 284   MORNING

Today I celebrate myself and my achievement. I look into my mirror and say what I feel:

_____

_____

_____

DAY 284   BEDTIME

Today has been the two-hundred-eighty-fourth day of my new smoke-free life. I look into my mirror and say what I feel:

_____

_____

_____

_____

_____   _____

Today's date   My signature

Continue to Build . . .
Your First Year
—Smoke-Free Log—

DAY 285   MORNING

Today I celebrate myself and my achievement. I look into my mirror and say what I feel:

_____

_____

_____

DAY 285   BEDTIME

Today has been the two-hundred-eighty-fifth day of my new smoke-free life. I look into my mirror and say what I feel:

_____

_____

_____

_____

_____   _____
Today's date   My signature

DAY 286   MORNING

Today I celebrate myself and my achievement. I look into my mirror and say what I feel:

_____

_____

_____

DAY 286   BEDTIME

Today has been the two-hundred-eighty-sixth day of my new smoke-free life. I look into my mirror and say what I feel:

_____

_____

_____

_____

_____   _____
Today's date   My signature

Continue to Build . . .
Your First Year
—Smoke-Free Log—

DAY 287   MORNING

Today I celebrate myself and my achievement. I look into my mirror and say what I feel:

_____

_____

_____

DAY 287   BEDTIME

Today has been the two-hundred-eighty-seventh day of my new smoke-free life. I look into my mirror and say what I feel:

_____

_____

_____

_____

_____   _____
Today's date   My signature

DAY 288   MORNING

Today I celebrate myself and my achievement. I look into my mirror and say what I feel:

_____

_____

_____

DAY 288   BEDTIME

Today has been the two-hundred-eighty-eighth day of my new smoke-free life. I look into my mirror and say what I feel:

_____

_____

_____

_____

_____   _____
Today's date   My signature

Continue to Build . . .
Your First Year
—Smoke-Free Log—

DAY 289   MORNING

Today I celebrate myself and my achievement. I look into my mirror and say what I feel:

_____

_____

_____

DAY 289   BEDTIME

Today has been the two-hundred-eighty-ninth day of my new smoke-free life. I look into my mirror and say what I feel:

_____

_____

_____

_____

_____   _____
Today's date   My signature

DAY 290   MORNING

Today I celebrate myself and my achievement. I look into my mirror and say what I feel:

_____

_____

_____

DAY 290   BEDTIME

Today has been the two-hundred-ninetieth day of my new smoke-free life. I look into my mirror and say what I feel:

_____

_____

_____

_____

_____   _____
Today's date   My signature

Continue to Build . . .
Your First Year
—Smoke-Free Log—

DAY 291   MORNING

Today I celebrate myself and my achievement. I look into my mirror and say what I feel:

_____

_____

_____

DAY 291   BEDTIME

Today has been the two-hundred-ninety-first day of my new smoke-free life. I look into my mirror and say what I feel:

_____

_____

_____

_____

_____   _____

Today's date   My signature

DAY 292   MORNING

Today I celebrate myself and my achievement. I look into my mirror and say what I feel:

_____

_____

_____

DAY 292   BEDTIME

Today has been the two-hundred-ninety-second day of my new smoke-free life. I look into my mirror and say what I feel:

_____

_____

_____

_____

_____   _____

Today's date   My signature

Continue to Build . . .
Your First Year
—Smoke-Free Log—

DAY 293   MORNING
Today I celebrate myself and my achievement. I look into my mirror and say what I feel:

_____

_____

_____

DAY 293   BEDTIME
Today has been the two-hundred-ninety-third day of my new smoke-free life. I look into my mirror and say what I feel:

_____

_____

_____

_____

_____

_____   _____

Today's date   My signature

DAY 294   MORNING
Today I celebrate myself and my achievement. I look into my mirror and say what I feel:

_____

_____

_____

DAY 294   BEDTIME
Today has been the two-hundred-ninety-fourth day of my new smoke-free life. I look into my mirror and say what I feel:

_____

_____

_____

_____

_____

_____   _____

Today's date   My signature

Continue to Build . . .
Your First Year
—Smoke-Free Log—

DAY 295   MORNING

Today I celebrate myself and my achievement. I look into my mirror and say what I feel:

_____

_____

_____

DAY 295   BEDTIME

Today has been the two-hundred-ninety-fifth day of my new smoke-free life. I look into my mirror and say what I feel:

_____

_____

_____

_____

_____   _____

Today's date   My signature

DAY 296   MORNING

Today I celebrate myself and my achievement. I look into my mirror and say what I feel:

_____

_____

_____

DAY 296   BEDTIME

Today has been the two-hundred-ninety-sixth day of my new smoke-free life. I look into my mirror and say what I feel:

_____

_____

_____

_____

_____   _____

Today's date   My signature

Continue to Build . . .
Your First Year
—Smoke-Free Log—

DAY 297   MORNING
Today I celebrate myself and my achievement. I look into my mirror and say what I feel:

_____

_____

_____

DAY 297   BEDTIME
Today has been the two-hundred-ninety-seventh day of my new smoke-free life. I look into my mirror and say what I feel:

_____

_____

_____

_____

_____   _____
Today's date   My signature

DAY 298   MORNING
Today I celebrate myself and my achievement. I look into my mirror and say what I feel:

_____

_____

_____

DAY 298   BEDTIME
Today has been the two-hundred-ninety-eighth day of my new smoke-free life. I look into my mirror and say what I feel:

_____

_____

_____

_____

_____   _____
Today's date   My signature

Continue to Build . . .
Your First Year
—Smoke-Free Log—

DAY 299   MORNING
Today I celebrate myself and my achievement. I look into my mirror and say what I feel:

_____

_____

_____

DAY 299   BEDTIME
Today has been the two-hundred-ninety-ninth day of my new smoke-free life. I look into my mirror and say what I feel:

_____

_____

_____

_____

_____   _____
Today's date   My signature

DAY 300   MORNING
Today I celebrate myself and my achievement. I look into my mirror and say what I feel:

_____

_____

_____

DAY 300   BEDTIME
Today has been the three-hundredth day of my new smoke-free life. I look into my mirror and say what I feel:

_____

_____

_____

_____

_____   _____
Today's date   My signature

Continue to Build . . .
Your First Year
—Smoke-Free Log—

DAY 301   MORNING

Today I celebrate myself and my achievement. I look into my mirror and say what I feel:

_____

_____

_____

DAY 301   BEDTIME

Today has been the three-hundred-first day of my new smoke-free life. I look into my mirror and say what I feel:

_____

_____

_____

_____

_____   _____

Today's date   My signature

DAY 302   MORNING

Today I celebrate myself and my achievement. I look into my mirror and say what I feel:

_____

_____

_____

DAY 302   BEDTIME

Today has been the three-hundred-second day of my new smoke-free life. I look into my mirror and say what I feel:

_____

_____

_____

_____

_____   _____

Today's date   My signature

Continue to Build . . .
Your First Year
—Smoke-Free Log—

DAY 303   MORNING
Today I celebrate myself and my achievement. I look into my mirror and say what I feel:

_____

_____

_____

DAY 303   BEDTIME
Today has been the three-hundred-third day of my new smoke-free life. I look into my mirror and say what I feel:

_____

_____

_____

_____

_____   _____
Today's date   My signature

DAY 304   MORNING
Today I celebrate myself and my achievement. I look into my mirror and say what I feel:

_____

_____

_____

DAY 304   BEDTIME
Today has been the three-hundred-fourth day of my new smoke-free life. I look into my mirror and say what I feel:

_____

_____

_____

_____   _____
Today's date   My signature

Continue to Build . . .
Your First Year
—Smoke-Free Log—

DAY 305 MORNING

Today I celebrate myself and my achievement. I look into my mirror and say what I feel:

_____

_____

_____

DAY 305 BEDTIME

Today has been the three-hundred-fifth day of my new smoke-free life. I look into my mirror and say what I feel:

_____

_____

_____

_____

_____   _____
Today's date   My signature

DAY 306 MORNING

Today I celebrate myself and my achievement. I look into my mirror and say what I feel:

_____

_____

DAY 306 BEDTIME

Today has been the three-hundred-sixth day of my new smoke-free life. I look into my mirror and say what I feel:

_____

_____

_____

_____   _____
Today's date   My signature

Continue to Build . . .
Your First Year
—Smoke-Free Log—

DAY 307   MORNING

Today I celebrate myself and my achievement. I look into my mirror and say what I feel:

_____

_____

_____

DAY 307   BEDTIME

Today has been the three-hundred-seventh day of my new smoke-free life. I look into my mirror and say what I feel:

_____

_____

_____

_____

_____   _____

Today's date   My signature

DAY 308   MORNING

Today I celebrate myself and my achievement. I look into my mirror and say what I feel:

_____

_____

_____

DAY 308   BEDTIME

Today has been the three-hundred-eighth day of my new smoke-free life. I look into my mirror and say what I feel:

_____

_____

_____

_____

_____   _____

Today's date   My signature

Continue to Build...
Your First Year
—Smoke-Free Log—

DAY 309   MORNING

Today I celebrate myself and my achievement. I look into my mirror and say what I feel:

_____

_____

_____

DAY 309   BEDTIME

Today has been the three-hundred-ninth day of my new smoke-free life. I look into my mirror and say what I feel:

_____

_____

_____

_____

_____   _____

Today's date   My signature

DAY 310   MORNING

Today I celebrate myself and my achievement. I look into my mirror and say what I feel:

_____

_____

_____

DAY 310   BEDTIME

Today has been the three-hundred-tenth day of my new smoke-free life. I look into my mirror and say what I feel:

_____

_____

_____

_____

_____   _____

Today's date   My signature

Continue to Build . . .
Your First Year
—Smoke-Free Log—

DAY 311   MORNING

Today I celebrate myself and my achievement. I look into my mirror and say what I feel:

_____

_____

DAY 311   BEDTIME

Today has been the three-hundred-eleventh day of my new smoke-free life. I look into my mirror and say what I feel:

_____

_____

_____

_____

_____   _____

Today's date   My signature

DAY 312   MORNING

Today I celebrate myself and my achievement. I look into my mirror and say what I feel:

_____

_____

DAY 312   BEDTIME

Today has been the three-hundred-twelfth day of my new smoke-free life. I look into my mirror and say what I feel:

_____

_____

_____

_____

_____   _____

Today's date   My signature

Continue to Build . . .
Your First Year
—Smoke-Free Log—

DAY 313   MORNING
Today I celebrate myself and my achievement. I look into my mirror and say what I feel:

_____

_____

_____

DAY 313   BEDTIME
Today has been the three-hundred-thirteenth day of my new smoke-free life. I look into my mirror and say what I feel:

_____

_____

_____

_____

_____   _____
Today's date   My signature

DAY 314   MORNING
Today I celebrate myself and my achievement. I look into my mirror and say what I feel:

_____

_____

_____

DAY 314   BEDTIME
Today has been the three-hundred-fourteenth day of my new smoke-free life. I look into my mirror and say what I feel:

_____

_____

_____

_____

_____   _____
Today's date   My signature

Continue to Build . . .
Your First Year
—Smoke-Free Log—

DAY 315   MORNING

Today I celebrate myself and my achievement. I look into my mirror and say what I feel:

_____

_____

DAY 315   BEDTIME

Today has been the three-hundred-fifteenth day of my new smoke-free life. I look into my mirror and say what I feel:

_____

_____

_____

_____

_____   _____

Today's date   My signature

DAY 316   MORNING

Today I celebrate myself and my achievement. I look into my mirror and say what I feel:

_____

_____

DAY 316   BEDTIME

Today has been the three-hundred-sixteenth day of my new smoke-free life. I look into my mirror and say what I feel:

_____

_____

_____

_____

_____   _____

Today's date   My signature

Continue to Build . . .
Your First Year
—Smoke-Free Log—

DAY 317   MORNING
Today I celebrate myself and my achievement. I look into my mirror and say what I feel:

_____

_____

_____

DAY 317   BEDTIME
Today has been the three-hundred-seventeenth day of my new smoke-free life. I look into my mirror and say what I feel:

_____

_____

_____

_____

_____   _____
Today's date   My signature

DAY 318   MORNING
Today I celebrate myself and my achievement. I look into my mirror and say what I feel:

_____

_____

_____

DAY 318   BEDTIME
Today has been the three-hundred-eighteenth day of my new smoke-free life. I look into my mirror and say what I feel:

_____

_____

_____

_____

_____   _____
Today's date   My signature

Continue to Build . . .
Your First Year
—Smoke-Free Log—

DAY 319   MORNING
Today I celebrate myself and my achievement. I look into my mirror and say what I feel:

_____

_____

_____

DAY 319   BEDTIME
Today has been the three-hundred-nineteenth day of my new smoke-free life. I look into my mirror and say what I feel:

_____

_____

_____

_____

_____   _____
Today's date   My signature

DAY 320   MORNING
Today I celebrate myself and my achievement. I look into my mirror and say what I feel:

_____

_____

_____

DAY 320   BEDTIME
Today has been the three-hundred-twentieth day of my new smoke-free life. I look into my mirror and say what I feel:

_____

_____

_____

_____   _____
Today's date   My signature

Continue to Build . . .
Your First Year
—Smoke-Free Log—

DAY 321   MORNING
Today I celebrate myself and my achievement. I look into my mirror and say what I feel:

_____

_____

_____

DAY 321   BEDTIME
Today has been the three-hundred-twenty-first day of my new smoke-free life. I look into my mirror and say what I feel:

_____

_____

_____

_____

_____   _____
Today's date   My signature

DAY 322   MORNING
Today I celebrate myself and my achievement. I look into my mirror and say what I feel:

_____

_____

_____

DAY 322   BEDTIME
Today has been the three-hundred-twenty-second day of my new smoke-free life. I look into my mirror and say what I feel:

_____

_____

_____

_____

_____   _____
Today's date   My signature

Continue to Build . . .
Your First Year
—Smoke-Free Log—

DAY 323   MORNING
Today I celebrate myself and my achievement. I look into my mirror and say what I feel:

_____

_____

_____

DAY 323   BEDTIME
Today has been the three-hundred-twenty-third day of my new smoke-free life. I look into my mirror and say what I feel:

_____

_____

_____

_____

_____   _____

Today's date   My signature

DAY 324   MORNING
Today I celebrate myself and my achievement. I look into my mirror and say what I feel:

_____

_____

_____

DAY 324   BEDTIME
Today has been the three-hundred-twenty-fourth day of my new smoke-free life. I look into my mirror and say what I feel:

_____

_____

_____

_____

_____   _____

Today's date   My signature

Continue to Build . . .
Your First Year
—Smoke-Free Log—

DAY 325   MORNING
Today I celebrate myself and my achievement. I look into my mirror and say what I feel:

_____

_____

_____

DAY 325   BEDTIME
Today has been the three-hundred-twenty-fifth day of my new smoke-free life. I look into my mirror and say what I feel:

_____

_____

_____

_____

_____   _____

Today's date   My signature

DAY 326   MORNING
Today I celebrate myself and my achievement. I look into my mirror and say what I feel:

_____

_____

_____

DAY 326   BEDTIME
Today has been the three-hundred-twenty-sixth day of my new smoke-free life. I look into my mirror and say what I feel:

_____

_____

_____

_____

_____   _____

Today's date   My signature

Continue to Build . . .
Your First Year
—Smoke-Free Log—

DAY 327   MORNING

Today I celebrate myself and my achievement. I look into my mirror and say what I feel:

DAY 327   BEDTIME

Today has been the three-hundred-twenty-seventh day of my new smoke-free life. I look into my mirror and say what I feel:

Today's date   My signature

DAY 328   MORNING

Today I celebrate myself and my achievement. I look into my mirror and say what I feel:

DAY 328   BEDTIME

Today has been the three-hundred-twenty-eighth day of my new smoke-free life. I look into my mirror and say what I feel:

Today's date   My signature

Continue to Build . . .
Your First Year
—Smoke-Free Log—

DAY 329   MORNING
Today I celebrate myself and my achievement. I look into my mirror and say what I feel:

_____

_____

_____

DAY 329   BEDTIME
Today has been the three-hundred-twenty-ninth day of my new smoke-free life. I look into my mirror and say what I feel:

_____

_____

_____

_____

_____   _____

Today's date   My signature

DAY 330   MORNING
Today I celebrate myself and my achievement. I look into my mirror and say what I feel:

_____

_____

_____

DAY 330   BEDTIME
Today has been the three-hundred-thirtieth day of my new smoke-free life. I look into my mirror and say what I feel:

_____

_____

_____

_____

_____   _____

Today's date   My signature

Continue to Build . . .
Your First Year
—Smoke-Free Log—

DAY 331   MORNING

Today I celebrate myself and my achievement. I look into my mirror and say what I feel:

DAY 331   BEDTIME

Today has been the three-hundred-thirty-first day of my new smoke-free life. I look into my mirror and say what I feel:

Today's date   My signature

DAY 332   MORNING

Today I celebrate myself and my achievement. I look into my mirror and say what I feel:

DAY 332   BEDTIME

Today has been the three-hundred-thirty-second day of my new smoke-free life. I look into my mirror and say what I feel:

Today's date   My signature

Continue to Build . . .
Your First Year
—Smoke-Free Log—

DAY 333   MORNING

Today I celebrate myself and my achievement. I look into my mirror and say what I feel:

_____

_____

_____

DAY 333   BEDTIME

Today has been the three-hundred-thirty-third day of my new smoke-free life. I look into my mirror and say what I feel:

_____

_____

_____

_____

_____   _____

Today's date   My signature

DAY 334   MORNING

Today I celebrate myself and my achievement. I look into my mirror and say what I feel:

_____

_____

_____

DAY 334   BEDTIME

Today has been the three-hundred-thirty-fourth day of my new smoke-free life. I look into my mirror and say what I feel:

_____

_____

_____

_____

_____   _____

Today's date   My signature

Continue to Build . . .
Your First Year
—Smoke-Free Log—

DAY 335   MORNING
Today I celebrate myself and my achievement. I look into my mirror and say what I feel:

_____

_____

DAY 335   BEDTIME
Today has been the three-hundred-thirty-fifth day of my new smoke-free life. I look into my mirror and say what I feel:

_____

_____

_____

_____

_____   _____

Today's date   My signature

DAY 336   MORNING
Today I celebrate myself and my achievement. I look into my mirror and say what I feel:

_____

_____

DAY 336   BEDTIME
Today has been the three-hundred-thirty-sixth day of my new smoke-free life. I look into my mirror and say what I feel:

_____

_____

_____

_____

_____   _____

Today's date   My signature

Continue to Build . . .
Your First Year
—Smoke-Free Log—

DAY 337   MORNING
Today I celebrate myself and my achievement. I look into my mirror and say what I feel:

_____

_____

_____

DAY 337   BEDTIME
Today has been the three-hundred-thirty-seventh day of my new smoke-free life. I look into my mirror and say what I feel:

_____

_____

_____

_____

_____   _____
Today's date   My signature

DAY 338   MORNING
Today I celebrate myself and my achievement. I look into my mirror and say what I feel:

_____

_____

_____

DAY 338   BEDTIME
Today has been the three-hundred-thirty-eighth day of my new smoke-free life. I look into my mirror and say what I feel:

_____

_____

_____

_____

_____   _____
Today's date   My signature

Continue to Build . . .
Your First Year
—Smoke-Free Log—

DAY 339   MORNING

Today I celebrate myself and my achievement. I look into my mirror and say what I feel:

_____

_____

_____

DAY 339   BEDTIME

Today has been the three-hundred-thirty-ninth day of my new smoke-free life. I look into my mirror and say what I feel:

_____

_____

_____

_____

_____   _____
Today's date   My signature

DAY 340   MORNING

Today I celebrate myself and my achievement. I look into my mirror and say what I feel:

_____

_____

_____

DAY 340   BEDTIME

Today has been the three-hundred-fortieth day of my new smoke-free life. I look into my mirror and say what I feel:

_____

_____

_____

_____

_____   _____
Today's date   My signature

Continue to Build . . .
Your First Year
—Smoke-Free Log—

DAY 341   MORNING
Today I celebrate myself and my achievement. I look into my mirror and say what I feel:

_____
_____
_____

DAY 341   BEDTIME
Today has been the three-hundred-forty-first day of my new smoke-free life. I look into my mirror and say what I feel:

_____
_____
_____
_____

_____   _____
Today's date   My signature

DAY 342   MORNING
Today I celebrate myself and my achievement. I look into my mirror and say what I feel:

_____
_____
_____

DAY 342   BEDTIME
Today has been the three-hundred-forty-second day of my new smoke-free life. I look into my mirror and say what I feel:

_____
_____
_____
_____

_____   _____
Today's date   My signature

Continue to Build . . .
Your First Year
—Smoke-Free Log—

DAY 343   MORNING

Today I celebrate myself and my achievement. I look into my mirror and say what I feel:

_____

_____

_____

DAY 343   BEDTIME

Today has been the three-hundred-forty-third day of my new smoke-free life. I look into my mirror and say what I feel:

_____

_____

_____

_____

_____   _____

Today's date   My signature

DAY 344   MORNING

Today I celebrate myself and my achievement. I look into my mirror and say what I feel:

_____

_____

_____

DAY 344   BEDTIME

Today has been the three-hundred-forty-fourth day of my new smoke-free life. I look into my mirror and say what I feel:

_____

_____

_____

_____

_____   _____

Today's date   My signature

Continue to Build . . .
Your First Year
—Smoke-Free Log—

DAY 345 MORNING

Today I celebrate myself and my achievement. I look into my mirror and say what I feel:

_____

_____

_____

DAY 345 BEDTIME

Today has been the three-hundred-forty-fifth day of my new smoke-free life. I look into my mirror and say what I feel:

_____

_____

_____

_____

_____   _____

Today's date   My signature

DAY 346 MORNING

Today I celebrate myself and my achievement. I look into my mirror and say what I feel:

_____

_____

_____

DAY 346 BEDTIME

Today has been the three-hundred-forty-sixth day of my new smoke-free life. I look into my mirror and say what I feel:

_____

_____

_____

_____

_____   _____

Today's date   My signature

Continue to Build . . .
Your First Year
—Smoke-Free Log—

DAY 347   MORNING
Today I celebrate myself and my achievement. I look into my mirror and say what I feel:

_____

_____
_____

DAY 347   BEDTIME
Today has been the three-hundred-forty-seventh day of my new smoke-free life. I look into my mirror and say what I feel:

_____

_____
_____
_____

_____   _____
Today's date   My signature

DAY 348   MORNING
Today I celebrate myself and my achievement. I look into my mirror and say what I feel:

_____

_____
_____

DAY 348   BEDTIME
Today has been the three-hundred-forty-eighth day of my new smoke-free life. I look into my mirror and say what I feel:

_____

_____
_____
_____

_____   _____
Today's date   My signature

Continue to Build . . .
Your First Year
—Smoke-Free Log—

DAY 349   MORNING
Today I celebrate myself and my achievement. I look into my mirror and say what I feel:

_____

_____

_____

DAY 349   BEDTIME
Today has been the three-hundred-forty-ninth day of my new smoke-free life. I look into my mirror and say what I feel:

_____

_____

_____

_____

_____   _____
Today's date   My signature

DAY 350   MORNING
Today I celebrate myself and my achievement. I look into my mirror and say what I feel:

_____

_____

_____

DAY 350   BEDTIME
Today has been the three-hundred-fiftieth day of my new smoke-free life. I look into my mirror and say what I feel:

_____

_____

_____

_____

_____   _____
Today's date   My signature

Continue to Build . . .
Your First Year
—Smoke-Free Log—

DAY 351   MORNING
Today I celebrate myself and my achievement. I look into my mirror and say what I feel:

_____

_____

_____

DAY 351   BEDTIME
Today has been the three-hundred-fifty-first day of my new smoke-free life. I look into my mirror and say what I feel:

_____

_____

_____

_____

_____   _____
Today's date   My signature

DAY 352   MORNING
Today I celebrate myself and my achievement. I look into my mirror and say what I feel:

_____

_____

_____

DAY 352   BEDTIME
Today has been the three-hundred-fifty-second day of my new smoke-free life. I look into my mirror and say what I feel:

_____

_____

_____

_____

_____   _____
Today's date   My signature

Continue to Build . . .
Your First Year
—Smoke-Free Log—

DAY 353   MORNING
Today I celebrate myself and my achievement. I look into my mirror and say what I feel:

_____

_____

_____

DAY 353   BEDTIME
Today has been the three-hundred-fifty-third day of my new smoke-free life. I look into my mirror and say what I feel:

_____

_____

_____

_____

_____   _____
Today's date   My signature

DAY 354   MORNING
Today I celebrate myself and my achievement. I look into my mirror and say what I feel:

_____

_____

_____

DAY 354   BEDTIME
Today has been the three-hundred-fifty-fourth day of my new smoke-free life. I look into my mirror and say what I feel:

_____

_____

_____

_____

_____   _____
Today's date   My signature

Continue to Build . . .
Your First Year
—Smoke-Free Log—

DAY 355   MORNING
Today I celebrate myself and my achievement. I look into my mirror and say what I feel:

_____

_____

DAY 355   BEDTIME
Today has been the three-hundred-fifty-fifth day of my new smoke-free life. I look into my mirror and say what I feel:

_____

_____

_____

_____   _____
Today's date   My signature

DAY 356   MORNING
Today I celebrate myself and my achievement. I look into my mirror and say what I feel:

_____

_____

DAY 356   BEDTIME
Today has been the three-hundred-fifty-sixth day of my new smoke-free life. I look into my mirror and say what I feel:

_____

_____

_____

_____   _____
Today's date   My signature

Continue to Build . . .
Your First Year
—Smoke-Free Log—

DAY 357   MORNING

Today I celebrate myself and my achievement. I look into my mirror and say what I feel:

_____

_____

_____

DAY 357   BEDTIME

Today has been the three-hundred-fifty-seventh day of my new smoke-free life. I look into my mirror and say what I feel:

_____

_____

_____

_____

_____   _____
Today's date   My signature

DAY 358   MORNING

Today I celebrate myself and my achievement. I look into my mirror and say what I feel:

_____

_____

_____

DAY 358   BEDTIME

Today has been the three-hundred-fifty-eighth day of my new smoke-free life. I look into my mirror and say what I feel:

_____

_____

_____

_____

_____   _____
Today's date   My signature

Continue to Build . . .
Your First Year
—Smoke-Free Log—

DAY 359   MORNING

Today I celebrate myself and my achievement. I look into my mirror and say what I feel:

_____

_____

DAY 359   BEDTIME

Today has been the three-hundred-fifty-ninth day of my new smoke-free life. I look into my mirror and say what I feel:

_____

_____

_____

_____

_____   _____
Today's date   My signature

DAY 360   MORNING

Today I celebrate myself and my achievement. I look into my mirror and say what I feel:

_____

_____

DAY 360   BEDTIME

Today has been the three-hundred-sixtieth day of my new smoke-free life. I look into my mirror and say what I feel:

_____

_____

_____

_____

_____   _____
Today's date   My signature

Continue to Build . . .
Your First Year
—Smoke-Free Log—

DAY 361   MORNING

Today I celebrate myself and my achievement. I look into my mirror and say what I feel:

_____

_____

_____

DAY 361   BEDTIME

Today has been the three-hundred-sixty-first day of my new smoke-free life. I look into my mirror and say what I feel:

_____

_____

_____

_____

_____   _____

Today's date   My signature

DAY 362   MORNING

Today I celebrate myself and my achievement. I look into my mirror and say what I feel:

_____

_____

_____

DAY 362   BEDTIME

Today has been the three-hundred-sixty-second day of my new smoke-free life. I look into my mirror and say what I feel:

_____

_____

_____

_____

_____   _____

Today's date   My signature

Continue to Build . . .
Your First Year
—Smoke-Free Log—

DAY 363   MORNING

Today I celebrate myself and my achievement. I look into my mirror and say what I feel:

_____

_____

_____

DAY 363   BEDTIME

Today has been the three-hundred-sixty-third day of my new smoke-free life. I look into my mirror and say what I feel:

_____

_____

_____

_____

_____   _____

Today's date   My signature

DAY 364   MORNING

Today I celebrate myself and my achievement. I look into my mirror and say what I feel:

_____

_____

_____

DAY 364   BEDTIME

Today has been the three-hundred-sixty-fourth day of my new smoke-free life. I look into my mirror and say what I feel:

_____

_____

_____

_____

_____   _____

Today's date   My signature

Continue to Build . . .
Your First Year
—Smoke-Free Log—

DAY 365   MORNING

Today I celebrate myself and my achievement. I look into my mirror and say what I feel:

_____

_____

_____

DAY 365   BEDTIME

Today has been the three-hundred-sixty-fifth day of my new smoke-free life. I look into my mirror and say what I feel:

_____

_____

_____

_____

_____   _____

Today's date   My signature

Congratulations
on your achievement of
One Year
of your new
Smoke-Free Life!

If you wish to continue a daily log,
use this book as a guide and do so; if not, continue to

"Stay Real"

regarding your arrested addiction to tobacco.

You can continue to utilize the tools in this book as you see fit in order to comfortably maintain your freedom from nicotine addiction, *for life*.

And may you have a long and healthy life!

Again, congratulations and best wishes to you.

Yours truly in Smoke-Free Living,

Jim Christopher

Clear Horizons:
Smoke-Free Potpourri

"**E**xcuse me," I said repeatedly over the last few years of my smoking, "I'm going outside for a cigarette." Now, at last, I can *stay put*: in my theater seat, at the dining room table, or anywhere else. There's smoke-free live activity.

And—

After having the greatest sex ever, my lover now hands me . . . a piece of luscious, ripe fruit, to share in the afterglow.

Or—

Following an exceptionally delicious meal, feeling stuffed and oh-so-satisfied, I immediately reach for . . . a glass of water and a few after-dinner mints. I no longer feel that "something is missing" without a cigarette.

Dudley-Do-Rightism? I think not. An authentic addiction-free life has less baggage, fewer regrets. Life's little pleasures—both naughty and nice—need not include sucking carbon monoxide from a paper tube.

There's so much out there besides smoking! I opined similarly when I first experienced freedom from alcohol addiction, over two decades ago. What I expressed then—regarding release from alcohol addiction—is true today, with slight modification, as applied to nicotine addiction. I've never met a smoker who *chose* to become an addict. . . . When addiction set in, for all of us, it was the equalizer.

In our new smoke-free lives we can and should be very good to ourselves. We can pursue our dreams, work toward our goals, partake in life's numerous nicotine-free pleasures and experiences. We feel better now than when we were smoking, why not look the part as well? Lose those surplus pounds. If your hairline is receding, why not get a transplant? Buy a new wardrobe. Work out in a gym. Travel. Start a new relationship. Reasonable hedonism has its place. Why not cherish these new years and relish the tobacco-free times of our lives?

You will begin to feel better about yourself and more attractive to others if you take the time to pamper yourself. Buy new clothing; visit a beautician or barber; wear makeup, perfume, or aftershave; get a facial or massage; wear expensive or formal clothing occasionally; join a health club; visit a sauna; get your teeth cleaned or fixed; buy new glasses; improve your diet.

You may find conversation difficult in your early days of recovery, but the topics available are virtually limitless: sports, philosophy, your health, your children or grandchildren, sex, politics, current events, religion, people, your job or schoolwork. Don't be afraid to ask for advice or help, to argue, or to be assertive or stubborn. You may even begin to like talking to others so much that you will decide to take up public speaking or lecturing.

There are many activities and events you can enjoy without

smoking. They include attending concerts, operas, ballets, plays, weddings, graduations, bar mitzvahs, social or civic club meetings, government meetings, court sessions, lectures, banquets, luncheons, school reunions, and alumni meetings. You can go to a fair, carnival, circus, amusement arcade, zoo, park, picnic, barbecue, museum or exhibit, a movie or drive-in, and the library. Attend auctions and garage sales, go shopping, or just go downtown and mingle. Many events are free and you can learn while being entertained.

Be creative! At one time you may have been interested in pursuing the arts but let your talents fall by the wayside. Or perhaps you have always wanted to try your hand at painting, drawing, sculpture, acting, movie-making, composing or arranging music, creative writing, singing, or playing a musical instrument. Now is the time!

Take up a sport: softball, baseball, basketball, football, boating, tennis, waterskiing, bowling, wrestling, boxing, fishing, horseback riding, badminton, shuffleboard, croquet, horseshoes, ping-pong, snowmobiling, swimming, running, jogging, gymnastics, aerobics, frisbee, catch, soccer, rugby, skiing, lacrosse, hockey, bicycling, handball, paddleball, squash, surfing, and scuba diving are just a few of the sports available. If you do not think you are physically capable of one of these, try cards, chess, checkers, board games, or party games, or just attend a sporting event. Cheering your team as a spectator is often as much fun as active participation.

If all the activity becomes too much for you, there are many ways to rediscover nature. Go for a ride in the country, a hike in the mountains, or a stroll on the beach; watch wild animals; listen to the sounds of nature; look at the stars, sky, clouds, or a storm; smell a flower; walk barefoot; go birdwatching, beachcombing, or mountain climbing; gather natural objects such as rocks, driftwood, or wild food; take a field trip. If you live in a metropolitan area and cannot get away, become an "urban explorer": take a walk in the city and notice the unexpected oases of nature there; make a snowman; hang a bird-feeder in your backyard; buy an aquarium. Observing nature can be a peaceful experience in even the most crowded environments.

Learn a new craft or skill; restore antiques; refinish furniture; take up woodworking or carpentry; hone your mechanical skills; learn a foreign language or American Sign Language; make food or crafts to sell or give away; invent something; take up gardening, landscaping, or yard work; learn photography; try your hand at writing articles, essays, reports, or scholarly papers; become a gourmet cook; can, freeze, or preserve foods; rearrange or redecorate your room, house, or apartment; work with beads, leather, or fabrics; make pottery or jewelry; take up knitting, crocheting, sewing, or needlework; do a scientific experiment; repair something.

Spend time alone: write in a diary; stay up late; meditate or do yoga; read the newspaper, stories, poems, novels, plays, "how-to" books or articles, essays, comic books, academic or professional literature, or magazines; people watch; write letters, cards, and notes; care for houseplants; spend time with your pet; collect things; take a walk; sleep late or get up early; listen to music; visit a cemetery and remember a departed friend or relative; watch television; cry; do odd jobs around the house; enjoy the peace and quiet; think positively about the future; talk to yourself; solve a puzzle; think about someone you like; daydream; sing to yourself; listen to the radio; scream out your frustrations or anger; work on your finances; think about your problems.

Spend time with other people: make a new friend; travel in a group; become acquainted with a neighbor; visit old friends and reminisce; teach or coach someone; give a massage or backrub; do someone a favor; help with someone's problems; tell a joke to lift someone's spirits (and your own!); confess or apologize to someone you may have hurt; smile at people; express your love to someone; have tea, coffee, or soft drinks with friends; be with children; give or attend a party; go to a family reunion; have lunch or dinner with friends or associates; have a frank and open conversation; try to be outgoing at a gathering; go dancing; congratulate someone; go on a date; join an encounter or therapy group; enjoy physical contact with someone; introduce people to each other; give gifts, send letters, and make telephone calls; buy something for someone; meet someone of the opposite sex; loan something; counsel someone; compliment someone; join a fraternity or sorority; play a harmless practical joke; tell someone you need him or her.

You can do volunteer work; visit the sick, shut-ins, or people in trouble; work on a political campaign; protest something; join a neighborhood group; defend or protect someone; help stop fraud or abuse. Become more involved with your work: attend a business meeting, luncheon, or convention; give a speech or lecture; pay more attention to details; and when you are offered that raise or promotion, accept it with pride!

ᘓ ᘓ ᘓ

If ol' Pavlov comes a-callin' with stardust smoke serenades . . .

STOP.

BREATHE.

REMEMBER.

THINK.

STAY REAL.

Say, as would a *transformed* Frankenstein:

> **"SMOKE BAD!"**
> **"FRESH AIR GOOD!"**
> **"SMOKE BAD!"**
> **"NEW LIFE GOOD!"**
> **"SMOKE BAD!"**
> **"MY LIFE MINE!"**
> **"SMOKE BAD!"**
> **"MY LIFE MINE!"**

and *allow* yourself to feel whatever feelings you may feel.

🌿   🌿   🌿

When it comes to smoking . . .

DON'T COMPROMISE.

Say to yourself:

> "I don't smoke, no matter what!"
> "I can't smoke and get away with it!"
> "I want my freedom!"
> "I want my life!"

🌿   🌿   🌿

At this writing I'm into my sixth year of freedom from nicotine addiction. Not to indulge myself, but to take you into my life—with all its warts—for a few moments, in order to share with you the separate-issue recovery method working well, providing yours truly with an extraordinarily comfortable recovery, I'll proceed. Please take note that I did not say "extraordinarily comfortable life circumstances"; recovery can be approached as a *separate issue* from all else.

Beginning with my first cigarette-free day to the present time, I've not experienced a "hold-onto-the-railing" Pavlovian pull for a smoke. As far back as I can remember I've had a tendency toward melancholy. As a young man I thought often about and openly discussed the prospect of suicide. I was drinking heavily at the time. And I smoked. At age thirty-five, when I was at long last able to shake off the bondage of booze, my glass, so to speak, became as it had been frequently in childhood, half full rather than half empty, and sunlight once again frequently shone through me.

I "kept on keepin' on" through thick and thin, as my grandmother had long ago modeled to me. The face of adversity witnessed me churning out lots of lemonade, rather than merely wallowing among the lemons that life had, rather generously, bestowed upon me. I continued to smoke in sobriety, though only half as much as when I had smoked and drank in the past, but, as nicotine-country cowboys could attest, "it done the job." Positively thrilled at my state of sobriety versus feeling drugged, enslaved, trapped, I never really noticed the thin veil of cigarette smoke that ever so slightly obscured my perspectives, my feelings, my in-the-momentness of life.

I continued to smoke, smoke, smoke until age fifty. Today, although I am not entwined entirely in roses, I do smell their fragrance and realize their beauty, but there's a lemonade stand visible near me as well. My love life has proved less than promised, on numerous occasions. By American standards, I don't make a great deal of money.

Health threats loom as years roll on by. I have holes in my self-esteem, dark spots on some of my days. . . . I suppose my point is this: What has any of this to do with drinking alcohol or smoking cigarettes? To me, not a damn thing.

That, indeed, is the point. My separate-issue recovery, to date, hasn't been rocked by adversity, angst, pain, mania, terror, paranoia, betrayal, despair, anger, rage, or sadness. So again, I sincerely pose the query: What's a drink or a smoke got to do with any of this stuff? Addictive chemicals, including cigarettes, *will not* "fix it," as I, in my long-lived drug-free state, have had the luxury to *see* intellectually (as far as my limited intellect will carry me); moreover, I also *see* this emotionally, primitively, *limbically*, if you will.

I *see* as a weary researcher in a lab at long last *sees* in that special moment when he or she lifts the vial of discovery to the light and exclaims "aha!" I *see* as a true believer *sees* during a religious tent revival or secular political rally, tears streaming in revealed awareness. I *see* as individual audience members *see*, spellbound by greatness in performance art, momentarily transcended to a place of indescribable clarity, beauty, depth; the heart, soul, human spirit: emotional response, *synchronized* with the mental faculties fused in a special "knowing" of the total self. Heavy shit, no? Point being, this can all be yours for a price. The price is acceptance, equal billing and respect for your primitive self side by side with your frontal lobe smarts. "Getting real" about addiction can free you from addiction. Heartfelt affirmations impact the *total* you; use 'em. Do your "mirror work." My point is (yes, you *knew* it was coming): If someone as screwed up as yours truly can stop smoking as a separate issue from all else and stay stopped, so the hell can you!

※　　※　　※

In my work I've met thousands of alcoholics and other chemical dependents in recovery. The great majority of them smoked cigarettes. Research seems to bear this out; that is, heavy drinkers/drug users are, more often than not, heavy smokers, with—as in all matters—some exceptions.

The former smokers I've spoken with who've escaped from nicotine country—long ago or more recently—have done so, I have found, via various means: the taper or fading method (as presented in this book); the "cold turkey" or stop-at-once method, formal cessation treatment, "the patch," hypnosis, acupuncture, meditation, and so on. We can all learn from each other and the end result is the same: a mutual escape from nicotine country. Former smokers have lots of allies today. Former smokers and those who've never smoked are waiting to welcome newcomers into their ranks and to heartily support them. To a degree, the tides have turned, we've got the support and lots of it, at least in this country. They're still puffing with a vengeance overseas, as I can attest. After all, "tobacco interests" wish to continue to live in the manner to which they're accustomed.

🌿 🌿 🌿

Humans tend, as we know, to continue to do whatever they can do with impunity: The primordial self does whatever it can get away with to feel pleasure, which it interprets as survival, until it comes smack dab into direct contact with a barrier of immediate pain.

You can toss out "noble" motivations when it comes to the nitty-gritty: The addicted individual human organism knee-jerks its way on down the road of life. You can also arrest addictions and keep them arrested with full-body knowledge, that is, by "getting real" about the fact that you can't *really* get away with it and by reinforcing that liberating, protective "total self" truth. The results—whether you are "noble," "tightly wrapped," or "nutty as a fruitcake" (with "unresolved issues" oozing from every pore)—will be . . . *separate-issue arrest of addiction, comfortably felt, comfortably experienced.* Then—and only then—can you move on to address "unresolved issues" as best you can, or not, or some, or none. Most folks are not scoundrels, they are merely rascals. Some may even have a little nobility sloshing around, after cellular needs are met.

🌿   🌿   🌿

I feel pretty good most of the time, in spite of my sometimes melancholy proclivities, because I no longer smoke, and that removal of a physiological/emotional energy drainer frees me to feel far better than I did six years ago. But I couldn't comprehend it when I was "in it," so to speak. You couldn't tell me about the dangers of smoking. My "lizard self" needed its fix, and protected its turf against "those alien nonsmoking freaks."

As I say, my natural state of relative well-being today, even though I'm older, makes me feel younger. I fully realize that this can be swept away, via disease, calamity, etc. . . . . But NO ONE CAN TAKE AWAY MY ALREADY-LIVED SMOKE-FREE YEARS! Man, what a glorious feeling that is!

Eat your heart out, Bette.

🌿   🌿   🌿

I'll tell you a secret. Years ago, at age nineteen, about the time Kennedy was assassinated, I worked for a brief time in the camera department of a large retail general-merchandise store in downtown Fort Worth, Texas.

"Buddy," an older, lovable man who managed the department,

often asked me, "Goddamn it, Jim, gimme a cigarette?" as he would go on break, grinning gratefully back at me. He wheezed from chronic emphysema as he climbed the stairs each day to the employee lounge. His wife had forbidden him cigarettes, so he bummed them whenever he could. He was a thin, frail figure. A former air-force pilot, he still flew and taught flying on weekends.

I really liked Buddy. Who wouldn't? Perhaps seeing cigarettes in action, so to speak, motivated me. Who knows? In any event, I decided to stop smoking. I told no one, I just did it. For three days. Never entertained the idea again, until 1993.

My life experience is mine; I accept it.

I will say to you, however, as I said earlier today to Tom, a fellow sober alcoholic who read my first book a decade ago and thanked me today for my having written it, as he is celebrating a decade of sobriety, having begun his recovery at age twenty-five, "Congratulations!"

If this book can play even a tiny part in your triumphant escape from nicotine country, I am most gratified. You may be nineteen or ninety-one; this is your time to reclaim your life. Go for it!

🌿   🌿   🌿

In 1962, my old friend Brad, a fellow heavy smoker and heavy drinker, helped Bette Davis and Joan Crawford pull me, lit to the gills, back into an elevator descending to the ground level of the legendary club Twenty-One in downtown Manhattan. The occasion: Bette and Joan, along with other show-biz luminaries, graced a small party held at Twenty-One in honor of their new picture, *What Ever Happened to Baby Jane?* Bette's daughter B.D., who later wrote a "tell all" book about her mom, while Bette was still living, was there, as were numerous other familiar faces of that day. Brad had managed to finagle an invitation for us to this lavish soirée, after he'd also arranged "press passes" for us earlier that evening to Basin Street East, to see jazz great Peggy Lee. Bobby Darin (a vocalist of "Mack the Knife" fame), drunk, had heckled Miss Lee from his seat in the small club until she bade him join her on stage.

Anyway, we were in New York to promote the mock-up of a new college magazine I'd published and Brad had edited. We were there on a shoestring budget and Brad's formidable talents for persuasion had come in handy. Several years my senior, Brad was a chain-smoking, hard-drinking journalism grad from the University of Texas who'd traveled to the Big Apple sharing my dream of a new national magazine for the college market. Hell, I hadn't lasted my first year at UT: studies had interfered with my drinking. I had, instead, chosen to be an "entrepreneur." There we were at this star-studded party and I was—as I heard someone say once during a later drunken escapade in a large New Orleans nightclub—"snot-slingin' drunk."

Bette, chain smoking Camels and seated elegantly at a table with a prominent critic of the time whose name escapes me, said, as she thumbed through a copy of the prototype of *Collegia* that Brad had gotten into her hands (he'd also talked our way to her table), "Good pah-puh." Bette found our proposed magazine for the college youth, well printed on good stock, charming. Meanwhile, I was admittedly in and out of an alcoholic blackout, smoking and drinking like a fiend. I spent some of the evening collapsed on the toilet seat back in the men's room of that fabled club, gaining, losing, and regaining consciousness. I do recall that Bette was surprisingly warm to us, while Joan was cold as steel, an icy smile splitting her face. I relay this past adventure in order to illustrate that had I been a non-chemically dependent lad at the time, I might have had an opportunity to. . . . But that's done. What has happened to me since sobriety and since my escape from nicotine country has been the ability to experience drug-free, *fully realized* adventures, working with others around the world, aiding in their escape from their individual addictions.

For instance, in London in 1997, I spoke to a large group of teens and select members of Parliament in the Grand Committee Room of the House of Commons on the subject of the advantages of a drug-free lifestyle. "Whoa! Stop! Hold on just one goddamned minute," one might protest, "What's your Bette Davis NYC-teenage London crap got to do with me? I'm not a f--king drunk, never have been. Smoking didn't take you down, booze did. So where do cigarettes fit into your pathetic little tale? Huh?" Answer: Synergistically. Smoking cigarettes *didn't* cause me to pass out in the can at Twenty-One, nor did it cause me to get trapped in the doors of an elevator, but whether one wishes to face it or not, nicotine addiction plays a part in eroding our everyday lives, blunting our authentic actions and reactions. Oh, sure, I could have enjoyed the Twenty-One-Bette-Davis-Joan-Crawford experience while smoking cigarettes and drinking moderately or not at all, and I could have addressed those British teens with a straight face, touting the advantages of a life without drugs, then had a cigarette break afterward. OK. Fine.

But heed this:

I've *now* got a point of comparison. Cigarette smoking sucks. It won't obviously impact your day-to-day behavior, rather it impedes your ability to experience life authentically and to its fullest, quietly sapping your energy, eroding and compromising your health. Is that not insidious?

❧   ❧   ❧

Stimulating? Feels good? Enhances an already pleasurable event? Tops off a glorious experience? Fills a momentary void? One's little dependable sidekick in a package? **Get real!**

"OK," one might say, "I no longer smoke, but, truth be told, I'd love to get away with it, if only I could!" **Get real!**

When you really, I mean *really*, let yourself see nicotine addiction for what it is, you'll get appropriately disdainful, angry at the drug. It's exceedingly impactful to systematically destroy distorted inner-child/Frankenstein-brain-stem/limbic notions that try to convince you, "It really *is* great!" Is it? Did Hitler deserve to live after tenderly fondling Eva Braun's wee wee? NO. Who cares that he had a weak dad and monstrous mom? He fucked up, to the max. He used up his stamps. He, as Frankenstein might say, "Bad!" Analogously, dancing-in-the-breeze tobacco leaves are also "Bad!" if consumed by *Homo sapiens*. Get rid of your "old buddy." Renounce your euphoric-hit-delivering enslaver for what it is: a life-destroying, powerfully addictive drug. You can "masturbate your inner child" in numerous other "I-want-it-NOW!" ways that won't hurt you. You can feel *great* without nicotine. Say to the drug: "You are NOT my friend!" Real friends don't hook you in, to ultimately kill you. Real friends celebrate your freedom, they cheer you on in your positive endeavors; they have no desire to control your life, your energy, your authentic essence. So, divorce that nicotine! It's OK to damn the drug. It has no redeeming value to you whatsoever.

🌿   🌿   🌿

You know that group of "regulars" down at the donut shop. Usually (but not always) over forty, some of them retirees, smoking, swapping stories, slurping coffee, salivating over bearclaws. Pose to them the advent of a cigaretteless, lowered-fat, caffeine-free lifestyle, including moderate exercise, and they'd wheezingly proclaim "Life is short. Folks who don't have any fun, don't *really* live longer . . . it just *seems* longer . . . har (cough) har (cough)! Besides, I had an uncle, Uncle Fred. He outlived three wives and smoked three packs a day," etc.

Ever notice most of these clowns carry extra poundage and don't usually walk with a spring in their step? That *is* their choice. The cig-arette counter awaits, and the donut shop is open twenty-four hours.

Walking. Yeah, simply walking briskly on a sunlit morn. Nice, huh? Think about it. How magnificent this experience really is, health restored, lungs full of fresh air, a sense of well-being pumping through your brain. See the mailman on his route, a flock of birds in the dis-tance. Hear a dog barking in the background and the sweet sound of children's laughter. You're feeling even more exhilarated as you climb a bit upward, rounding the corner past a flower-filled vacant lot. Alive! "Yes," you say to yourself, "I am alive!"

"Hey, 'scuse me. Yeah, you. 'Scuse me, you got a cigarette?" And your easy reply, complete with internal smile: "No, I don't smoke."

Deb carries the bulk of two men. She meets regularly with other women. They kibitz, chain-smoke, and are at one with their food. They use a lot of tissues, because they're women with issues.

Tanya left the group, stopped smoking, dropped forty-seven pounds, frequently runs the distance of a nearby track, and recently enrolled in a junior college.

I know a lady who keeps her age a secret (she's eighty-five). She told me that she escaped from nicotine country decades ago (and she stopped drinking booze as well). Every day, she leaves the apartment building she has managed for many years, brightly dressed, ready to attack various projects. She'd been a heavy smoker and hadn't, she said, much energy left by the time she bid tobacco adieu.

If you think Sarah is a rarity, you'd be wrong, from what I've seen in the addiction-recovery field. Productive persons abound, having abandoned tobacco.

Sarah shared what happened to her last pack of cigarettes: She flushed them down the toilet.

      🌿   🌿   🌿

I remember Mom, on the way to church with Dad who was driving and smoking. She insisted he open the car window wider and I was gagging in the backseat. The '52 Chevy was sparkling black and brand-spanking new, our family pride. Dad joined other churchmen in the gravel lot outside the small white frame Texas Protestant tabernacle, and I hung out with them before services began.

Dad looked spiffy, I thought, and manly as he continued in lively banter with the other men, smokers all. My folks' hellfire-and-brimstone beliefs excluded smoking as a send-you-to-hell habit. Drinking (and dancing) were forbidden, the secret shame of some. But smoking . . . smoking was a staple in my life.

I have an earlier memory of being carried in a blanket to church, the smell of Dad's cigarette.

Many years later, Dad's drinking, although well hidden by both parents from me, became evident. Dad eventually stopped drinking about two decades prior to his death, continuing, however, to smoke till only a few years before he succumbed to a fatal heart attack.

Aunt Waynell was always, I recall, svelte. She ate heartily, giving no thought to the matter of her food intake. Relatives would say, "I wish I was like Waynell; she can eat *anything* and not gain weight!" That ain't me. I always had to deal with from eight to thirty pounds creeping up on me. Never much for strenuous exercise, I went on various diets over the years, off and on, since my late teens. I managed to stay between "ideal" and only about eight pounds over, most of the time; still a pain in the ass, though. Only when I stopped smoking and began a *nonoppressive*, virtually daily, exercise commitment, in conjunction with sensible but, again, *not oppressive* (respecting my "inner child," if you will) food choices and eating parameters, did I *comfortably maintain* my "ideal" weight.

My "cut-off valve" for hunger was always faulty, or perhaps it is more accurate to say that I pay more attention nowadays to appropriate hunger feelings, as opposed to "I feel nervous, sad, angry, bored (or whatever), sooo . . . let's eat!" *But,* since I'm careful to truly respect my "inner child" or primitive self, I make sure my food choices are satisfying and fun. Yes, fun. That is not to say that I live only to eat or that I continuously substitute food for feelings. Of course, I do that to some degree, but not to the degree that unwanted weight returns. No, I'm smarter with food intake now, more creative. And, as I said, it's fun for me, a nice part of life, not my focal point of life, to be sure, but a wonderful part.

For example, the vast majority of delicious dishes that I love, I recreate in lowered-fat versions. And, like many folks, I'm busy, *and* "I want it NOW!" on frequent occasion, so quick stir-fry fare minus oil in the preparation (using a little pan spray instead) works beautifully. An example: I simply toss in some frozen veggies, cooked shrimp, and seasonings, and voilà! a dish is ready in literally a matter of a few minutes. I also drink lots of nonalcoholic sparkling beverages, my favorites.

My point: I don't feel deprived with regard to food. I feel satisfied.

ᵥ   ᵥ   ᵥ

I've been utilizing an inexpensive plastic device for my daily stomach crunches since I purchased it via mail order some years ago, after viewing a television infomercial. About two years ago I saw my little plastic helper "trashed" on a TV "magazine show," along with numerous other stomach-crunch devices, by "fitness experts." So what? It works for me, individually, and that, I think, is a good point about moderate exercise: It should be tailored to the individual's needs.

Research tells us that daily moderate exercise is best and necessary, along with high-fiber, low-fat food parameters, to maintain good health and a healthy weight. I was never big on exercise. In fact, years earlier I loathed it. Sporadically I'd take an interest, then my interest would wane and back to the couch I'd go. And I smoked.

So, smoke-free and with more energy than the old days, I enjoy moderate, yes, sometimes vigorous, exercise. And my stamina! Did I mention that walking with other tourists on a lengthy foreign city tour, or hiking with other hikers, is actually fun now? Sometimes I marvel at this exhilarating stuff. Say, why don't we all march to "tobacco-industry headquarters" with torches and pitchforks and . . . just kidding.

ᵥ   ᵥ   ᵥ

Images. Countless films—and I'm an avid film buff—contain seemingly endless smoking scenes . . . elegant ladies and sophisticated gentlemen puff from extended cigarette holders in ancient films, rough-and-tumble types light one unfiltered cigarette after another. Lovers smoke in the forest, on a blanket . . . fade out. Now, I could interject, "They also cough up blood." Not necessarily. Smoking images are always with us, but what has any of this stuff got to do with me? I simply can't smoke and get away with it.

🌿   🌿   🌿

"I guess, in a way, cigarettes were a substitute for life." John cleared his throat, continuing, "I mean, they're stimulating. Right? Smoking is stimulating. And my life wasn't always particularly exciting. I guess boredom, yeah, to fill a space. It's . . . I don't miss cigarettes. I don't think about it very much."

Sally spoke. "John, you've been off for how long?"

"A little over six months."

Ted chimed in, "I kept stalling it. My doctor said that I had better stop now. That was about two years ago. Now I've got about 80 days off cigarettes. I feel good, though."

Rita added, "Ted, you come across to me as very calm. I'm 'officially' telling you guys that I'm right in the middle of my 'fading plan' and, so far, so good."

Larry popped the tab on a can of diet soda and said, "Rita, good luck! We'll be rooting for you! We're . . . none of us is superhuman here. So many people have stopped smoking. Knowing that helps me a lot. And, I'm also gonna beat this cancer thing! I haven't had the need to smoke for almost a year now."

🌿   🌿   🌿

I sincerely hope this little book has been of some help to you. I still marvel at the ease with which I was able to stop smoking comfortably and not gain weight in the process, and I hope the same holds true for you. But not only that; I also hope you'll experience a new sense of well-being, coupled with the priceless awareness of having reclaimed your life.

If you'd like to share your escape from nicotine country with me, simply send a letter to me. My address, once again, is:

Jim Christopher
ENC Groups
PO Box 9522
Marina del Rey CA 90295

Recommended Reading

American Council on Science and Health. *Cigarettes: What the Warning Label Doesn't Tell You.* Amherst, N.Y.: Prometheus Books, 1997. Original publication: New York: American Council on Science and Health, 1996.

Perhaps the finest, most detailed, best-researched, and most devastating analysis of all the multifold health consequences of "tobaccosis," the modern epidemic that has killed more than 100 million people worldwide. To quote from the foreword: "The American Council on Science and Health believes that in 1996 Americans—smokers and nonsmokers alike—have only the most cursory understanding of the extent and magnitude of the health risks associated with cigarette smoking as opposed with other alleged health risks in the environment." *Strongly recommended!*

Bellerson, Karen J. *The Complete and Up-to-Date Fat Book: A Guide to the Fat, Calories, and Fat Percentages in Your Food.* Garden City Park, N.Y.: Avery Publishing Group, 1993.

Another excellent book whose title says it all.

Carper, Jean. *Jean Carper's Total Nutrition Guide.* New York: Bantam Books, 1987.

An excellent book on nutrition, nutrients, nutritional guidelines, and suggestions on the proper preparation of foods. As the cover says, "Based on the U.S. Department of Agriculture's new ten-year scientific study of the nutritional content of food."

Cornacchia, Harold J., and Stephen Barrett. *Consumer Health: A Guide to Intelligent Decisions.* 5th ed. Saint Louis, Mo.: Mosby-Year Book, 1993.

This is an up-to-date textbook on all aspects of health care, along with substantive criticisms of various fads, frauds, and other nonscientific health care. To quote from the forward: "You can gain a great deal from this book if you're interested in nutrition, physical fitness, body-building, high-level wellness, choosing trustworthy health-care professionals, avoiding health rip-offs, getting more for your health dollar."

Fletcher, Anne M. *Eating Thin for Life: Food Secrets & Recipes from People Who Have Lost Weight & Kept It Off.* Shelburne, Vt.: Chapters Publishing, 1997.

Anne Fletcher's best-selling book has deserved the praises that have been showered upon it. Well researched and an excellent read.

Gullo, Stephen P. *Thin Tastes Better: Control Your Food Triggers without Feeling Deprived.* New York: Dell Publishing, 1995.

This sensible alternative to dieting is one of my favorites. Learn to prepare healthful foods that taste at least as good as the typical dishes you already like, and that give you the same satisfaction.

Schmitz, Joy M., Nina G. Schneider, and Murray E. Jarvik. "Nicotine." In *Substance Abuse: A Comprehensive Textbook.* 3d ed. Edited by Joyce H. Lowinson, et al. Baltimore: Williams & Wilkins, 1997, pp. 276–94.

This is an excellent summary of the medical effects of nicotine as well as the various methods of cessation. It concludes with a lengthy bibliography.

The following articles were not written for popular audiences, but are highly technical and written for professionals.

Berecz, J. M. "Superiority of a Low-Contrast Smoking-Cessation Method." *Addictive Behaviors* 9, no. 3 (1984): 273–78.

Contrasts a group who practiced nicotine-fading with number-fading treatments, with the former being superior. Also focuses on the correlation of caffeine and alcohol intake with cigarette smoking.

Foxx, R. M., and E. Axelroth. "Nicotine Fading Self-Monitoring and Cigarette Fading to Produce Cigarette Abstinence or Controlled Smoking." *Behaviour Research and Therapy* 21, no. 1 (1983): 17–27; *Journal of Applied Behavior Analysis* 12, no. 1 (spring 1979): 111–25.

Thirty-eight subjects were assigned to four different fading techniques. An 18-month follow-up showed that nicotine fading/self monitoring was the most successful strategy in this particular test, with a 40 percent abstinence rate.

Garcia, Becona E., M.P. "Nicotine Fading and Smokeholding Methods to Smoking Cessation." *Psychological Reports* **73, no. 3, part 1 (December 1993): 779–86.**

Results of tests of five variations on fading techniques, showing that the most effective method was a combination of nicotine fading and cigarette fading, with an abstinence rate, a year after the completion of the test, of 57 percent.

Lando, H. A., and P. G. McGovern. "Nicotine Fading as a Non-aversive Alternative in a Broad-Spectrum Treatment for Eliminating Smoking." *Addictive Behaviors* **10, no. 2 (1985): 153–61.**

Comparison of oversmoking, nicotine fading, nicotine fading/smokeholding, and a nonmaintenance control. Though no method was largely successful in this test, the "absolute outcome for nicotine fading/smokeholding was encouraging. This procedure is both safe and apparently very acceptable to subjects. If the current results can be replicated, a clinically effective technique will have been established with applicability in both clinic and self-help settings."

McGovern, P. G., and H. A. Lando. "Reduced Nicotine Exposure and Abstinence Outcome in Two Nicotine-Fading Methods." *Addictive Behaviors* **16, nos. 1–2 (1991): 11–20.**

Results of tests of two variations on fading techniques. Here the best results came from the use of graduated filters.

Molimard, M., and A. Hirsch. "Methods of Stopping Smoking." *Revue de maladies respiratoires* 7, no. 4 (1990): 307–12. (Note: This article is in French.)

A test of various cessation methods (individual therapy, group therapy, medication, etc.) for people who were unable to quit smoking on their own. The results here show that patient motivation seems more important than the particular therapy used. Summarizes the need to reduce social pressures to smoke.

SOS International Clearinghouse, 5519 Grosvenor Boulevard, Los Angeles, CA 90066; tel. (310) 821–8430, fax (310) 821–2610.

Those of you who are also interested in dealing with alcohol and other drug problems should find this group helpful. I founded SOS in the 1980s; it now has meetings throughout the world and is a recognized alternative to Alcoholics Anonymous. I have authored three books detailing the SOS approach to sobriety: *How to Stay Sober, Unhooked,* and *SOS Sobriety.*

Stop-Smoking Support Page

REPRINTED, BY PERMISSION, FROM WWW.UNHOOKED.COM,
MARTIN NICOLAUS, WEBMASTER

Introduction

Most alcoholics or drug addicts have several addictions, and smoking is the most common other addiction by far.

Many alcoholics in recovery do not realize that their cigarette smoking is probably an even greater threat to their health and survival than their drinking was. Did you know that more alcoholics die of diseases related to smoking than of diseases related to drinking?

Before the 1930s, treatment of alcoholism and drug addiction commonly also included treatment of nicotine addiction. Smoking was generally viewed as a contributing factor in alcohol and drug relapses. But with the rise of Alcoholics Anonymous (AA), concern with smoking as a recovery issue faded into the background. Bill W., the co-founder of AA, was a chainsmoker who died of emphysema. Today, the treatment industry and the recovery community are returning to the original positions. Smoking is recognized as a drug addiction on par with other substance addictions, and is being treated accordingly.

For many alcoholics, smoking is a behavioral and chemical trigger for drinking, and getting clean from cigarettes is a major step toward reducing cravings for alcohol. Many alcoholics in recovery have successfully quit smoking after they quit drinking. Studies have shown also that alcoholics can quit drinking and smoking at the same time, and modern treatment centers are increasingly based on this principle.

For the recovering alcoholic even more than for the ordinary smoker, kicking cigarettes may be a question of life or death. **If you're an alcoholic or drug addict in recovery who wants to quit smoking—no matter when or how—this page is a page of support for YOU.**

Drinking and Puffing Go Together

You knew this already?

- More than 90 percent of alcoholics smoke, compared to about a third of nonalcoholics.
- Alcoholics smoke more cigarettes per day than do nonalcoholic smokers.
- Alcoholics are more likely to smoke mentholated cigarettes.

- The number of cigarettes a person consumes rises in tandem with the number of drinks consumed.
- Almost every smoker who smokes more than two packs a day is also an alcoholic.

Source: T. Bien and R. Barge, "Smoking and Drinking:
A Review of the Literature" (1990),
International Journal of the Addictions *25, no. 12.*

Smoking Kills More Drunks Than Drinking

WESTPORT, Apr 10 (Reuters)—More alcoholic individuals die from tobacco-related diseases than from alcoholism, according to a report in this week's JAMA. Mayo Clinic investigators led by Dr. Richard D. Hurt reviewed the records of 845 persons admitted to an inpatient-addiction program for treatment of alcoholism and dependence on other non-nicotine drugs between 1972 and 1983.

On initial hospital admission, 75 percent of the patients listed themselves as current cigarette smokers, 8 percent were former smokers, and 3 percent smoked pipes or cigars. In 1994, Dr. Hurt's team checked the program's records to determine the current status of those patients and to obtain death certificates for any who had died.

Death certificates obtained for 214 of the 222 deceased patients indicated that the cause of death was tobacco-related in 50 percent, and alcohol-related in 34 percent. Dr. Hurt says the cumulative mortality from smoking among substance abusers was 48.1 percent, about 2 times the expected rate. This suggests to Dr. Hurt that most persons undergoing treatment for alcoholism should undergo treatment for nicotine dependence as well.

Source: Journal of the American Medical Association
276 (1996), pp. 1097–1103.

For example, Bill W.

"Bill W. was lifted to the podium in his wheelchair, oxygen tank at his side. He was dying of lung disease. A brave, relentless visionary gave his last professional address about alcohol dependency, only to die from lung disease related to cigarette smoking. He died from nicotine addiction."

Source: Marlene, M. Maheu, Ph.D., "Recovery Community:
Have We Let Smoke Get in Our Eyes?"

Facts about Nicotine Addiction

"Tobacco use is addicting and nicotine is the active pharmacologic agent of tobacco that causes addictive behavior. It also causes physical dependence characterized by a withdrawal syndrome that usually accompanies nicotine abstinence. Evidence about the addictive nature of nicotine has been accumulating since 1942 when a medical researcher first identified the problem.

"Since that time many medical writers and journals have unequivocally classed smoking, and particularly cigarette smoking, as an addiction for many people. Some physicians compare the addictive qualities of nicotine to heroin and barbiturates, but others maintain that for many people cigarettes can be even more addictive than heroin, barbiturates, or alcohol. . . .

"The 1988 Surgeon General's report, 'The Health Consequences of Smoking: Nicotine Addiction,' found that nicotine is a powerful pharamacologic agent that acts in the brain and throughout the body. Nicotine readily crosses the blood-brain barrier and accumulates in the brain shortly after it enters the body. Once in the brain it interacts with specific receptors and alters brain energy metabolism in a pattern consistent with the distribution of specific binding sites for the drug."

Source: ASH—Action on Smoking and Health

For a comprehensive and up-to-date summary of current scientific knowledge about smoking, see *Research Report on Nicotine Addiction* (1998) by the National Institute on Drug Abuse (NIDA).

Smoking Is Like Drinking with the Lungs

More recent research has turned up an additional chemical in tobacco smoke that directly interferes with the brain's chemical reward systems in the same way as other addictive drugs. In a recently reported study (*Nature* 379 [1996], pp. 733–736), a team of researchers from Brookhaven National Laboratory in Upton, New York, found that the brains of living smokers have markedly less of the enzyme monoamine oxidase B (MAO B) compared with the brains of nonsmokers or former smokers.

MAO B (one of two isozyme forms of the enzyme) is involved in breaking down dopamine, a neurotransmitter that plays a role in movement as well as in feelings of pleasure, including those associated with most substances of abuse, including cocaine, amphetamines, heroin, alcohol, and nicotine.

The finding, researchers, say, may help explain the strong association found between smoking and depression. It also suggests that cigarettes are a "gateway drug" to other addictive substances, since the effects in the brain are analogous.

The findings also cast doubt on much previous addiction research. Because most substance abusers smoke, "it's very difficult to sort out what effects are caused by smoking and what effects are caused by the abused substance," said chemist Joanna S. Fowler, Ph.D., one of the authors of the study.

—Based on Joan Stephenson, Ph.D., in the
Journal of the American Medical Association *(April 24, 1996).*

Withdrawal Symptoms Like with Drugs

When rats were given nicotine for a week and then it was withdrawn, their brains registered a 40 percent drop in response to pleasure stimuli for periods lasting from several days to as long as two weeks. These brain changes "rival the magnitude and duration of similar changes observed during withdrawal from other abused drugs such as cocaine, opiates, amphetamines, and alcohol," according to a new study funded by the National Institute on Drug Abuse (NIDA), and published in *Nature*, May 7, 1998.

Eh, What?

Oh, and a recent medical study shows that among many other harms, smoking is associated with increased risk of hearing loss.

Source: The Journal of the American Medical Association
(June 3, 1998).

The Treatment Industry Had a 50-Year Amnesia Gap about Nicotine Addiction

"The problem in most addictions-treatment programs at this time is that nicotine dependence is not addressed in the same way that other addictive disorders are treated. Historically, the early efforts at treatment of alcoholism by the Salvation Army did include treatment of nicotine dependence.

"Somewhere between then and the early 1960s when inpatient treatment programs began to develop, that concept was lost and the emphasis was on treating the alcoholism to the exclusion of other conditions. At that time, it was unlikely for alcoholics to be dependent on other drugs except nicotine. In the late 1970s and early 1980s, the demographics began to change and use of other drugs such as marijuana, cocaine, narcotics, sedatives, and tranquilizers was more commonly seen in alcoholic patients undergoing treatment.

"During this time of transition, the treatment community began incorporating the treatment for other drugs of dependence into their programs, except for nicotine. The major point of our study is that if the treatment community is concerned about the ultimate outcome for their patients (i.e., mortality), it is difficult to ignore nicotine dependence as a treatment issue."

Source: Richard D. Hurt, M.D., "Letters,"
Journal of the American Medical Association *(September 11, 1996).*

"Nineteenth- and early-twentieth-century inebriety specialists . . . waged a consistent attack on tobacco as a harmful and addictive substance and viewed smoking as a contributing factor in alcoholic and narcotic relapse. [But] modern addiction specialists took on the issue of tobacco only when the evidence of the harmfulness of smoking and the addictiveness of nicotine had become overwhelming. . . .

"By the late 1980s the addiction-treatment field was going through a rather painful process of self-examination and self-confrontation related to its response to the nicotine addiction of the majority of its workforce and clients. There were growing calls to look at the issue of smoking as an ethical as well as a clinical issue. Growing numbers of programs went smoke-free and began to state explicitly that they would hire only nonsmoking staff. Programs also began to combine treatment for smoking with the treatment for alcoholism and other drug addictions, and conduct these simultaneously."

Source: William L. White, Slaying the Dragon:
A History of Addiction Treatment and Recovery in America
(1998), pp. 309–310.

"In the past, substance-abuse programs have been reluctant to intervene on smoking due to presumed negative effects. Current evidence dispels these myths that have kept smoking interventions and other substance-abuse programs separate. Several studies have reported an overwhelmingly favorable response to implementing concurrent intervention for nicotine and other substance dependence. . . . Data indicate that smoking-cessation programs can be delivered within the context of alcohol treatment without negative consequences. . . ."

*Source: Joy M. Schmitz, Nina G. Schneider, and Murray E. Jarvik,
in Lowinson, et al.,* Substance Abuse: A Comprehensive Textbook,
3rd ed. (1998), p. 286.

People Can and Do Quit Drinking and Smoking at the Same Time

"There is no research support for the contention that alcoholics should not try to quit smoking at the same time they are attempting to quit drinking. In fact, the research more closely supports the view that 'smoking and drinking are correlated behaviors; anything causing a reduction in one may be associated with a reduction in the other.'"

Source: T. Bien and R. Barge, "Smoking and Drinking:
A Review of the Literature" (1990),
International Journal of the Addictions *25, no. 12.*

Kaiser HMO Goes Smoke-Free

The Chemical Dependency Recovery Program at the Kaiser HMO in Oakland, California, announced October 1, 1998, that all its facilities would be tobacco-free, that all patients in its treatment programs would be encouraged to quit smoking, and that members would have to recite their tobacco-free time as well as their time clean and sober off other drugs. In a flyer handed out to all patients, Kaiser staff said, "We encourage all CDRP clients to discontinue smoking as nicotine is a mood- and mind-altering drug that is responsible for the majority of deaths among alcoholics and addicts."

There Are Many Ways to Stop Smoking

Unlike the alcoholism field, which is still dominated by the quasi-monopoly of AA with its religious 12 Steps, the field of smoking-cessation presents a wide-open smorgasbord of different approaches, practically all of them secular.

There are two broad branches, the pharmacological and the behaviorist. The "patch," the gum, the nasal spray, and the nicotine inhaler are methods of delivering nicotine to your system without smoking, on the theory that you will gradually wean off.

Use of such nicotine replacements is vastly more effective if done in combination with some kind of behavioral therapy. There are numerous behavioral approaches, often used together. Common ones include tapering or fading, scheduling or timing, motivational enhancements via rewards and punishments of different kinds, relapse prevention, cue exposure, aversion therapy, and others.

There are numerous other approaches as well: nutrition, hypnosis, acupuncture, herbal teas, you name it. There's undoubtedly a quantity of worthless and even harmful hype as well, so be alert. Some methods are done alone, some in groups. there are commercial programs, noncommercial programs, inpatient and outpatient programs, and there is a growing self-help literature.

There are not yet, apparently, any programs aimed specifically at the sober alcoholic or drug addict who wants to quit smoking. **But then, as a person who has successfully quit drinking and/or drugging, you already know a lot about addiction and you have a head start!**

Support Systems to Quit Smoking

Here is a sampling of resources for the person who wants to quit smoking:

Sober Stop-Smoking Support Group. Right here in the cyber community, there is a group of recovering alcoholics and drug addicts who are working at quitting smoking. A more understanding support group you could not ask for. Join the no-smoke e-mail support list.

tobaccofacts.org. A hard-hitting, fact-studded site by the government of British Columbia, Canada. Learn what's really in cigarette tobacco, and many other interesting resources.

Kickbutt.org. A web site of Washington, D.C., DOC (Doctors Ought to Care), with an extensive info section about nicotine addiction, links to numerous quit-smoking sites, and information about the tobacco industry.

Quitnet. Based in Boston, this is a many-faceted smoking-cessation resource site. Information, referrals, chats, other links, support by the ton.

American Lung Association. Their slogan is "When You Can't Breathe, Nothing Else Matters." They have stop-smoking support groups practically everywhere, and they know whereof they speak. Check your local Yellow Pages for a listing.

American Heart Association. Their web site has extensive information about the effects of smoking on the heart, plus good backgrounders on the tobacco industry and its influence and marketing practices.

Centers for Disease Control. Tobacco information and Prevention Source (TIPS). "Tobacco use remains the leading preventable cause of death in the U.S." With a page of information on how to quit, plus a broad range of smoking facts.

Unhooked.org. A web site (no relation to the "unhooked.com" site) dedicated to supporting people who want to quit smoking. Has nicotine facts, quit tips, nightly support chats, links to other resources.

alt.support.stop.smoking (AS3). A newsgroup where participants explore all aspects of the quit-smoking problem. The group's FAQ File contains a wealth of experience and resources; check it out. You may even get additional tools for staying sober here.

The Master Anti-Smoking Page. Sponsored by a stop-smoking software program for Windows, this modestly titled site has numerous tips and support links.

Action on Smoking and Health. This veteran legislative-action group's web site is filled with information about smoking, the tobacco industry, tobacco litigation, and related topics.

Tobacco BBS (Bulletin-Board System) is a free resource center focusing on tobacco and smoking issues. It features news, information, assistance for smokers trying to quit, alerts for tobacco-control advocates, and open debate on the wide spectrum of tobacco issues.

Ro's Smoke-Free Mountain is a support-group discussion list where people help each other to quit smoking and stay quit.

Oncolink: Smoking and Cancer. Maintained by the University of Pennsylvania Cancer Center.

Olivia's Chronic Obstructive Pulmonary Disease Page. If you didn't quit smoking until it was too late, here's a page of advice and support for dealing with issues such as lung-volume-reduction surgery, oxygen tanks, and living with COPD. Excellent lung-pathology slides here.

The Nicorette Home Page. Information by the makers of a brand of nicotine gum, patch, and other stop-smoking aids.

Smokenders. A commercial smoking-cessation program.